WHAT IS THE REAL
MARXIST TRADITION?

WHAT IS THE REAL
MARXIST TRADITION?

JOHN MOLYNEUX

Haymarket Books

Chicago, Illinois

WHAT IS THE REAL MARXIST TRADITION?
By John Molyneux

First published in 1985 by Bookmarks (London and Chicago).

This edition published in 2003 by Haymarket Books. The essay "Stalinism and Bolshevism" by Leon Trotsky was added to this edition.

PO Box 180165
Chicago, IL 60618 USA
www.haymarketbooks.org

Cover design by Eric Ruder / www.redrhinodesign.com

ISBN: 1-931859-07-8

Printed in Canada

HAYMARKET BOOKS is a project of the Center for Economic Research and Social Change, a nonprofit educational foundation.

We take inspiration—and our name—from the Haymarket Martyrs, who gave their lives fighting for a better world. Their struggle for the eight-hour day in 1886 gave us May Day, the international workers' holiday, a symbol for workers around the world that ordinary people can organize and struggle for their own liberation.

CONTENTS

This book is part of a series—the International Socialist tradition. This series aims to reaffirm and make available writings from the genuine socialist tradition of workers' self-emancipation and to rescue socialism from its detractors on both the right and left.

Other titles in the International Socialist tradition series:

Marxism and the Party
by John Molyneux

Party and Class
essays by Tony Cliff, Duncan Hallas, Chris Harman and Leon Trotsky

Russia: From Workers' State to State Capitalism
essays by Anthony Arnove, Peter Binns, Tony Cliff, Chris Harman and Ahmed Shawki

Part one
What is Marxism?

As in private life one distinguishes between what a man thinks
and says of himself and what he really is and does, still more
in historical struggles must one distinguish the phrases and
fancies of the parties from their real organism and their real
interests, their conception of themselves from their reality.
Karl Marx: **The 18th Brumaire of Louis Bonaparte**

'All I know,' said Marx, 'is that I'm not a Marxist.' What
in the 1870s was a neat dialectical joke has since been transformed into a major political problem. The one hundred years
since Marx's death have seen the emergence of innumerable
divergent and conflicting 'Marxisms'. The centenary of that
death seems an appropriate moment to attempt to untangle this
particular knot, to establish the criteria for accepting claims to
the title of Marxism and thus to answer the question 'What is
the genuine Marxist tradition?' But first let us be clear about the
dimensions of the problem.

It is not just that people who call themselves Marxists hold
different views on certain questions (say 'the tendency of the
rate of profit to fall' or the class nature of the Soviet Union): that
is something to be expected in any living democratic movement.
The real problem is that frequently the 'Marxists' are to be
found imprisoning, killing, and making war on each other, and,

more fundamentally, that in all the great social conflicts of our age self-proclaimed 'Marxists' are to be found on opposing sides of the revolutionary barricades. Think of Plekhanov and Lenin in 1917, of Kautsky and Luxemburg in 1919, of the Communists and the POUM in Barcelona in 1936, of Hungary in 1956 and of Poland in 1981. It is this which compels us to pose the question of what defines Marxism.

There are, of course, some who would reject the question altogether, denying that the search for a 'true' Marxism has any meaning and simply accepting as Marxist all those who claim the label. On the one hand this is a convenient response for the bourgeoisie and its cruder ideologists, in that it permits them to condemn all Marxism and Marxists by association with Joe Stalin and Pol Pot, the butcher of Cambodia. On the other hand it also suits the academic Marxologists, enabling them to produce numerous profitable 'guides to the Marxists', offering cribs to every school of thought from the Austro-Marxists to the Althusserians.

Such an approach is essentially contemplative. Action, especially political action, requires decisiveness in theory as well as practice. Marxists who want to change the world, not just to make a living from interpreting it, have no choice but to face the problem and to draw a dividing line between the genuine and the false.

One way of trying to draw such a dividing line might be to identify Marxism with the works of Marx and to measure the followers simply by their faithfulness to the word of the master. Again this is a scholastic, even religious, approach. It fails to take account of the fact that if Marxism is, as Engels said, 'not a dogma, but a guide to action', then it must be a living, developing theory, capable of continuous growth, which has to analyse and respond to an ever changing reality — a reality which has in fact changed enormously since Marx's day. Even if, for historical reasons, we name the theory after the individual who did most to establish it, we cannot, at the price of total impotence, reduce or confine it to what that individual himself wrote. As Trotsky observed, 'Marxism is above all a method of analysis — not analysis of texts but analysis of social relations.'[1]

This quotation from Trotsky points in the direction of an alternative solution to the problem — one adopted by Hungarian

Marxist George Lukacs. In **History and Class Consciousness** Lukacs asked 'What is Orthodox Marxism?' and answered as follows:

> Orthodox Marxism . . . does not imply the uncritical acceptance of the results of Marx's investigations. It is not the 'belief' in this or that thesis, nor the exegesis of a 'sacred' book. On the contrary, orthodoxy refers exclusively to method.[2]

This is a much more serious proposal in that it takes account of the need for development, and it contains an important element of truth in that the dialectical method is without doubt central to Marxism. Nonetheless it is inadequate as a solution to our problem. It is not possible to establish such a rigid demarcation between Marx's method and his other analyses, nor to reduce the essential contents of Marxism solely to method.[3] This is shown by the very example Lukacs gives to illustrate his proposition.

> Let us assume [writes Lukacs] for the sake of argument that recent research had disproved once and for all every one of Marx's individual theses. Even if this were to be proved, every serious 'orthodox' Marxist would still be able to accept all such modern findings without reservation and hence dismiss all of Marx's theses *in toto* — without having to renounce his orthodoxy for a single moment.[4]

Quite the contrary is the case. If, for example, in defiance of Marx's whole analysis of the dynamic of capitalist development, capitalism were to evolve into a new form of world bureaucratic society without internal competition and contradictions, which precluded the possibility of either socialism or barbarism, then Marxism would clearly be refuted, and the proponents of such a perspective — Max Weber, Bruno Rizzi and James Burnham — would be vindicated. As Trotsky concluded when considering this hypothetical perspective, 'nothing else would remain except only to recognise that the socialist programme, based on the internal contradictions of capitalist society, ended as a Utopia.'[5]

What the foregoing argument might seem to suggest is that Marxism should be defined as a method *combined with* certain essential analyses and propositions. But this apparent solution in reality only pushes the problem one stage back. By what criterion can it be decided which analyses and propositions are fundamental and which are secondary? Moreover such an approach bears with it the danger of theoretical sectarianism, of defining Marxism as 'the correct line on everything', and so arriving at the position that Luxemburg was not a Marxist when she disagreed with Lenin about the party, that Lenin was not a Marxist when he maintained the bourgeois nature of the Russian Revolution, and so on.

How then can we break out of this circle? Not by first seeking to extract from Marx's work certain theses, but by using Marxist theory to view Marxism as a totality.

1
The class basis of Marxism

For Marx 'It is not social consciousness that determines social being, but social being that determines social consciousness.'[6] Consequently the understanding and definition of any philosophy, theory, or ideology is first and foremost a matter of disclosing the 'social being' that constitutes its foundation.

Thus Marx treats religion in general as 'the self-consciousness and self-awareness of man who either has not yet attained to himself or has already lost himself again.'[7] 'This state, this society,' he writes, 'produces religion's inverted attitude to the world, because they are an inverted world themselves.'[8] He reveals the earthly family as the secret of the Holy Family.[9] Similarly Engels analyses early Christianity as 'the religion of slaves and emancipated slaves . . . of peoples subjugated or dispersed by Rome.'[10]

In the **Communist Manifesto** Marx defines the various existing schools of 'socialism' directly by reference to the class interests they represent, giving us in turn feudal socialism, petty-bourgeois socialism, bourgeois socialism and so on. And, at a later date, Trotsky showed that the key to fascist ideology as well as the fascist movement lay in the class position of the petty-bourgeois crushed between capital and labour. These examples can be multiplied indefinitely; the point is that the same method of analysis must be applied to Marxism itself —

and this of course was the procedure of Marx and Engels themselves.

Engels begins **Anti-Dühring** with the assertion that 'Modern socialism is, in its content, primarily the product of the recognition, on the one hand, of the class antagonisms prevailing in modern society between proprietors and non-proprietors, between capitalists and wage-workers, and on the other, of the anarchy ruling in production.'[11] We can complete Engels' formulation by adding that Marxism is the recognition of these contradictions from the point of view of the proletariat, the industrial working class. As Marx puts in in **The Poverty of Philosophy**, 'Just as the economists are the scientific representatives of the bourgeois class, so the Socialists and Communists are the theoreticians of the proletarian class.'[12] And in the **Communist Manifesto**: 'The theoretical conclusions of the Communists are in no way based on ideas or principles that have been invented, or discovered, by this or that would-be universal reformer. They merely express, in general terms, actual relations springing from an existing class struggle, from an historical movement going on under our very eyes.'[13]

Also in the **Communist Manifesto** is the following immensely important passage:

> The Communists are distinguished from the other working-class parties by this only: 1. In the national struggles of the proletarians of the different countries, they point out and bring to the front the common interests of the entire proletariat, independently of all nationality. 2. In the various stages of the development which the struggle of the working class against the bourgeoisie has to pass through, they always and everywhere represent the interests of the movement as a whole.[14]

This amplifies and clarifies the definition of Marxism as the theory of the working class, establishing that what is involved is the articulation of the interests not of this or that section of the class but of the working class as a whole regardless of nationality — and today we might add of race or of sex. It thereby serves as the starting point for the identification and criticism of opportunism, at the root of which lies the sacrifice of the overall interests of the class to the temporary interests of particular national, local or craft groups within it.

What we have proposed is not only a social but also an

historical definition. Such a definition also explains why Marxism arose when it did. Exploitation and oppression existed for thousands of years and capitalism in its early forms for centuries, but Marxism could not emerge until capitalism had developed the productive forces, and therewith the proletariat, to the point where the latter's potential to overthrow capitalism could be perceived. We should note that Marx arrived at Marxism only on the basis of his contact with revolutionary workers' circles in Paris in late 1843. It was then that Marx discovered 'the formation of a class with radical chains', and first declared his allegiance to the proletariat. When the proletariat 'proclaims the dissolution of the hitherto existing world order,' wrote Marx at the time, 'it merely declares the secret of its own existence, since it is in fact the dissolution of this order.'[15]

This approach to the origins of Marxism differs markedly from that offered by Kautsky and taken up by Lenin in **What Is To Be Done?** as part of his argument that socialism must be introduced into the working class 'from without'. Kautsky wrote that 'socialism and the class struggle arise side by side and not one out of the other . . . the vehicle of science is not the proletariat but the bourgeois intelligentsia'[16] and Lenin argued that 'in Russia, the theoretical doctrine of social democracy arose altogether independently of the spontaneous growth of the working class movement; it arose as a natural and inevitable outcome of the development of thought among the revolutionary socialist intelligentsia.'[17] I have attempted elsewhere[18] to refute this position, to show its harmful consequences, and to demonstrate that it was characteristic of Lenin's thought only up to his experience of the revolutionary working class in 1905. Suffice it to say here that the Kautsky-Lenin theory is an example of the contemplative materialism criticised by Marx in the **Theses on Feuerbach**, and that, in the **Communist Manifesto**, Marx offers his own explanation of the role of the socialist intelligentsia. A section of the ruling class, 'in particular a portion of the bourgeois ideologists who have raised themselves to the level of comprehending theoretically the historical movement as a whole', cuts itself adrift and 'goes over to the proletariat'.[19] Clearly one cannot 'go over' to a class which is not in existence and which has not yet made its presence felt in the battle — as was the case with the Russian working class at the time Kautsky and Lenin were considering.

Finally, when considering the class basis of Marxism, it is necessary to emphasise that Marxism is not just the theory of the proletariat's resistance to capitalism and its struggle against capitalism; it is also, and above all, the theory of its victory. This point was made by Marx himself when he disclaimed all credit for discovering classes and class struggle:

> Long before me bourgeois historians had described the histori-
> cal development of this class struggle and bourgeois economists
> the economic anatomy of the classes. What I did that was new
> was to prove: (1) that the existence of classes is only bound up
> with particular historical phases in the development, (2) that
> the class struggle necessarily leads to the dictatorship of the
> proletariat, (3) that this dictatorship itself only constitutes the
> transition to the abolition of all classes and to a classless society.[20]

And the same point is made with even greater force by Lenin when, in **The State and Revolution**, he insists that, 'A Marxist is solely someone who extends the recognition of the class struggle to the recognition of the dictatorship of the proletariat . . . This is the touchstone on which the real understanding and recognition of Marxism should be tested.[21] Lenin's assertion was directed above all at Kautsky, who had spent decades presenting himself as the last word in Marxist orthodoxy yet turned his back on the actual workers' revolution in Russia. However, it retains all its relevance today when there is no shortage of intellectuals 'interested in', or even adhering to, Marxism as a method of interpreting society but who show no interest at all in the theory, still less the practice, of the struggle for workers' power.

Thus far, analysis of Marxism as the theory of the proletariat has shown that this conception contains three elements; Marxism as the theory of the common interests of the entire class internationally; Marxism as the product of the birth of the modern proletariat and the developments of its struggle against capitalism; Marxism as the theory of the victory of that class. The definition that most succinctly summarises these elements is that Marxism is *the theory of the international proletarian revolution*.

2
The scientific status of Marxism

To many people the definition of Marxism as the theory of a particular social class is incompatible with its claims to be scientific. The argument runs both ways. On the one hand there are those who recognise Marxism to be based on a definite social group and consequently deny its status as science. The foremost representative of this position is the sociologist Karl Mannheim.[22] On the other hand there are those who proclaim Marxism as science and therefore deny that it derives from the standpoint of the proletariat. The most important contemporary proponent of this view is Althusser, for whom such a definition reduces Marxism to 'the level of ideology'. These objections are the product of a double confusion: first as to the nature of natural science, second as to the relationship between natural science and social science.

Natural science is seen as providing exact, 'objective' and non-socially determined knowledge, and therefore is held to be the model for 'objective' social science. But this view of natural science is itself a social product. In the last analysis it derives from the alliance between science and the bourgeoisie which was necessary for the battle against feudalism and for the development of modern manufacturing. Just as the bourgeoisie depicted the laws of capitalism as natural and eternal so it depicted the achievements of science as absolute truth. The history of science, however, shows it to consist of a series of provisional relative truths which are produced under the stimulus of developing practical human needs, and which in turn demonstrate their truth in practice, by making possible the performance of definite tasks.[23] Natural science is therefore not absolute but historical and changing.

All social science, including Marxism, is, of course, subject to these same limitations, but there is also a fundamental difference between natural and social science. Natural science possesses an objectivity[24] which is not available to social science. There are two main reasons for this.

Firstly, knowledge is always a relationship between knower and known, between subject and object. In natural science the object of knowledge, nature, exists outside of human beings. Society however *is* human beings, the ensemble of human relations.[25] Nature and the laws of nature are not the creation of humanity. Society and social laws are. The world of nature can be altered by men and women but only on the basis of natural laws which cannot be altered. Social laws however can be changed.

The consequence of these differences is that all human beings stand in roughly the same relationship to the laws of nature but in markedly different relationships to the laws of society. Thus, as a result of the law of gravity, a worker and a capitalist dropped from the Leaning Tower of Pisa will strike the ground at the same speed and with the same consequences. The law of value however does not have the same consequences for the worker and the capitalist — it produces poverty for one and riches for the other. Which is why the idea of 'proletarian' as opposed to 'bourgeois' natural science is a piece of Stalinist nonsense.[26] But 'to expect [social] science to be impartial in a society of wage-slavery is as silly and naive as to expect impartiality from employers on the question of whether the worker's wages should be increased by decreasing the profits of capital'.[27]

Secondly, the purpose of knowledge is to assist in changing reality. This is equally true of natural and social science. The bourgeoisie has an interest in changing, indeed is continually compelled to change, the natural world in order to accumulate capital. It therefore needs natural science. In relation to society, however, the predominant interest of the bourgeoisie is not to change it but to preserve it as it is. Consequently the basic need of the bourgeoisie is not for social knowledge but for social apologetics, for ideology.[28]

Thus much of what passes for bourgeois social science is not science of any description. It is not practical or operational even for the bourgeoisie — but simply justification and mystification. Good examples are the marginal utility theory of value in economics and the pluralist theory of power in politics. Of course the bourgeoisie does need to change society within certain limits, the limits of the capitalist mode of production, and so bourgeois social science does yield a certain limited amount of real knowledge — knowledge which can also be used against capitalism. But this knowledge is always set within, and cramped and distorted by, a theoretical framework which obstructs real understanding of society as a whole. The only class which is both interested in, and capable of, arriving at an understanding of society as a totality, is the class that is interested in and capable of changing it as a totality — namely the proletariat. As Marx put it, 'The existence of revolutionary ideas in a particular period presupposes the existence of a revolutionary class.'[29]

Thus the class basis of Marxism, far from compromising its standing as science, is precisely what makes its scientific character possible.

A further argument against this view, really an extension of the argument considered above, is that it wrongly narrows down and limits the applicability of Marxism. This argument has been advanced by the older Lukacs. In his 1924 study of Lenin Lukacs began with the statement that 'Historical materialism is the theory of proletarian revolution',[30] but in his 1967 Postscript he dismisses this proposition as a product of 'the prejudices of the time' and protests at such an attempt 'to reduce to a single dimension and to cramp the real and methodological wealth — the social universality — of historical materialism, by such a definition.'[31]

This objection is false because the definition of Marxism as a class theory in no way restricts it to the analysis of just the proletarian struggle or even just capitalist society (though that is of course its central task). It is perfectly possible to analyse the whole of human history up to the present *from the standpoint of the proletariat*. Witness, for example, Engels' article on 'The

Part Played by Labour in the Transition from Ape to Man'. The central idea of this article is that labour 'is the prime basic condition of all human existence and . . . that, in a sense . . . labour created man himself.'[32] This could be arrived at only on the basis of an understanding of the labour of the modern working class,[33] and indeed *was* so derived for it is present in embryo in the **1844 Manuscripts** and **The German Ideology**,[34] before Marx and Engels had conducted any anthropological researches and before Darwin.

Moreover, in this same article Engels does not fail to point out the political conclusion that follows from his proposition — the necessity of 'a complete revolution in our hitherto existing mode of production'.[35] The 'social universality' demanded by Lukacs is possessed by Marxism precisely because it is based on the interests of the proletariat, the universal class — universal in the sense that it is the bearer of the future and liberation of all humanity, and in the sense that, needing neither a class above it to rule it nor a class below it to exploit, it can become all humanity. Lukacs' objection signifies not his broadened or deepened conception of Marxism but simply his own abandonment of a revolutionary class position through his absorption by Stalinism.

3
From practice to theory

To complete the argument that the essence of Marxism is that it is the theoretical expression of the proletarian revolution, it is necessary to demonstrate the connections leading from the conditions of existence of the proletariat and the tasks confronting it in the struggle (the social practice that *is* the proletariat) to the main propositions of Marxist theory. To do this comprehensively and rigorously is beyond the reach of this small book, all we can do is to trace the outline of some of the most important of these connections.

Let us begin with those aspects of Marxism that might be called its political principles and programme. Firstly, internationalism. There can be no doubt as to the central role played by internationalism in the thought of Marx, but Marxist internationalism owes nothing to an abstract moral (in reality bourgeois liberal) commitment to 'the international brotherhood of peoples'.[36] Rather it is grounded in the existence of the proletariat as an international class, created by the capitalist world market, and engaged in an international struggle against that system.

The statement in the **Communist Manifesto** that 'The working men have no country', and that 'national differences and antagonisms between people are daily more and more vanishing, owing to the development of the bourgeoisie, to freedom of commerce, to the world market, to uniformity in the modes of production and to the conditions of life corresponding thereto', has often been criticised as an exaggeration or an outright error, in the light of the continuing hold of nationalist ideology over the proletariat. Nonetheless it remains true at two levels. First as a statement of tendency rather than accomplished fact. Secondly as a statement about the proletariat relative to other social classes. The modes of production (and the cultures) of Japan, Brazil and Britain have infinitely more in common today than they did a century ago. In relation to the peasantry it was not even possible to speak seriously of international consciousness or organisation. The internationalism of the bourgeoisie, despite its creation of the world economy and its plethora of international organisations, remains qualitatively inferior to the international potential of the proletariat. The highest level it can rise to is the international bloc or alliance set against rival international blocs and even these are continually disrupted by national antagonisms.

The basic characteristic of Marxist internationalism is, as we have noted, the priority of the whole (the interests of the world working class) over the part. To make this more concrete: a revolutionary worker who has never left his home town, speaks only his native language, and yet opposes his 'own' government in time of war is far more of an internationalist than the learned professor who has travelled the world, speaks half a dozen languages, is steeped in the knowledge of different cultures, and yet in time of war supports his own government. Again, because of the priority of the whole, Marxist internationalism is perfectly compatible with recognition of the right to national self-determination and support for national liberation struggles, if the interests of the international class demand it.[37]

Secondly, take the principle of state ownership of the means of production. To many (especially the bourgeoisie, but also many would-be Marxists) this has been seen as the fundamental principle of Marxism and of socialism in general. Usually, when those who take this view are socialists, they reason as follows. Capitalism, which equals private ownership, is irrational and unjust, it causes economic crises, poverty, war etc. If production were state-owned and there was state planning of the economy, it would be an altogether better, more rational, arrangement and these evils would be ended. The struggle of the proletariat is then seen as a means by which this end can be achieved. Should an alternative means to this end present itself, say peasant guerrilla war or parliamentary legislation, then that makes no real difference.

Marxist reasoning is quite different. The proletariat is locked in class struggle against the bourgeoisie which exploits and oppresses it. The only way it can win that battle and emancipate itself is to defeat the bourgeoisie politically and take possession of the means of production. This it can do only by creating its own state. This is how the question is presented in the **Communist Manifesto**:

> We have seen above, that the first step in the revolution by the working class is to raise the proletariat to the position of ruling class, to win the battle of democracy. The proletariat will use its political supremacy to wrest, by degrees, all capital from the bourgeoisie, to centralize all instruments of production in the hands of the State, i.e. of the proletariat organized as the ruling class; and to increase the total of productive forces as rapidly as possible.

For the state socialists state ownership is the end, the working class the means. For Marxism the emancipation of the class is the end, state ownership the means. This difference — the 'two souls of socialism' as Hal Draper has called it — has been of immense significance in the past hundred years and we shall return to it repeatedly.

The ultimate aim of Marxism — the classless society — has of course been an age-old human aspiration. What distinguishes Marxism is that it derives the classless society, as a realistic possibility, from the development of the proletariat, 'a class which owing to its whole position in society, can only free itself by abolishing altogether all class rule, all servitude and all exploitation.'[38] To cite the **Communist Manifesto** again:

> All preceding classes that got the upper hand, sought to fortify their already acquired status by subjecting society at large to their conditions of appropriation. The proletarians cannot become masters of the productive forces of society except by abolishing their own previous mode of appropriation and thereby also every other previous mode of appropriation. They have nothing of their

own to secure and to fortify; their mission is to destroy all
previous securities for, and insurances of, individual property.

In terms of theory the transition from capitalism to communism — the dictatorship of the proletariat — was considered
to be (as we have noted) merely (!) the extension of the proletarian
class struggle to the point of victory. However, the specific form
of this dictatorship was discovered neither by Marx nor any other
Marxist theorist, but by revolutionary workers themselves. First
by the Parisian workers in the Commune of 1871, who showed
that rather than taking over the existing state machine it was
necessary to smash it, and whose actions indicated the first
principles of workers' democracy — payment of all officials at
workers' wages, election and recall of all delegates, replacement
of the standing army by the armed workers, etc. Second by the
workers of Petrograd (and then all Russia) who created the
organisational form uniquely suited to the expression of workers'
power — the soviet or workers' council. The great merit of the
soviet, it should be noted, is that it is based not on the worker as
individual citizen in a geographical area, but on the worker as
part of a collective in the workplace, the unit of production, and
that it arises within capitalism as a natural development of the
workers' struggle against capitalism — its historical point of
departure was an enlarged strike committee. It should also be
noted that Marxist theory on this question (Marx's **The Civil
War in France**, Lenin's **The State and Revolution**, Gramsci's
articles in **Ordine Nuovo**) is a direct generalisation of the most
advanced experience of the class.

Now we must turn from the programme of Marxism to its
theoretical foundations: the materialist conception of history and
the critical analysis of capitalism.

What is the basis of historical materialism? This question
can be approached analytically (by considering the concepts and
propositions of this theory) or historically (by tracing its genesis
and development in the works of Marx). Of these the analytic
approach is more important as the historical genesis of a theory
might include all sorts of accidental factors and detours.

Let us begin with the question of materialism versus
idealism.

Idealism — belief in the priority of mind ('spirit', 'ideals',
'God', etc.) over matter — and the idealist conception of history

(history as determined by the development of ideas, consciousness, etc.) has, itself, a material basis. It lies in the division between mental and manual labour and the emergence of a ruling class freed from manual labour, in other words living off the labour of others.

> Division of labour only becomes truly such from the moment when a division of material and mental labour appears. (The first form of ideologists, priests, is concurrent.) From this moment onwards consciousness can really flatter itself that it is something other than consciousness of existing practice, that it really represents something without representing something real; from now on consciousness is in a position to emancipate itself from the world and to proceed in the formation of 'pure' theory, theology, philosophy, ethics, etc.[39]

By contrast materialism is the 'natural' theory of a producing class struggling for its emancipation.[40] But of course we cannot simply identify historical materialism with materialism. Materialism preceded Marxism by more than two thousand years and in the eighteenth century materialism was the standpoint of the rising bourgeoisie. What distinguishes Marxist materialism from this bourgeois materialism? Marx expressed it thus:

> The chief defect of all hitherto existing materialism (that of Feuerbach included) is that the thing, reality, sensuousness, is conceived only in the form of the object of contemplation, but not as sensuous human activity, practice, not subjectively.[41]

In other words bourgeois materialism is mechanical. It treats human beings as passive, as mere products or effects of material circumstances — as objects. In doing so it reflects the actual position of men and women in capitalist society — the worker as an appendage of the machine, labour as a 'factor' of production equivalent to other factors (land, machines, etc.), living labour as subordinate to and a 'part' of dead labour. Mechanical materialism, however, is incapable of complete consistency; in consistent form it would be a total determinism and fatalism and it is impossible to act in the world on this basis. Therefore it always contains a more or less hidden exemption clause for itself whereby idealism re-enters through the back door, as the 'knowledge', 'science', or sometimes 'will' of the elite:

The materialist doctrine concerning the changing of circumstances and upbringing forgets that circumstances are changed by men and that it is essential to educate the educator himself. This doctrine must, therefore, divide society into two parts, one of which is superior to society.[42]

Marx overcame this antinomy through the concept of practice. 'The coincidence of the changing of circumstances and of human activity or self-changing can be conceived and rationally understood only as revolutionary practice.'[43] The model for this concept of practice was human labour, the means whereby humanity shapes and changes nature, and creates itself. Hegel's outstanding achievement, Marx writes:

. . . is, first, that Hegel grasps the self-creation of man as a process . . . and that he therefore grasps the nature of *labour*, and conceives objective man (true because real man) as the result of his *own labour*.[44]

But, Marx goes on, 'Labour as Hegel understands and recognises it is *abstract mental* labour.'[45] Marx was able to go beyond Hegel, to stand him on his feet and recognise labour as concrete practical activity as the basis of man and history ('this simple fact hitherto concealed by an overthrowth of ideology'[46]) because, and only because, he had before him in the proletariat the first class of immediate producers able to transform society and become its master. It is this conception of the role of labour, of production, that constitutes the methodological and empirical point of departure of the Marxist theory of history. From it are developed the key concepts of 'forces of production', 'relations of production' and 'mode of production' which in turn culminate in the theory of the social revolution:

In the social production of their life, men enter into definite relations that are indispensable and independent of their will, relations of production which correspond to a definite stage of development of their material productive forces. The sum total of these relations of production constitutes the economic structure of society, the real foundation, on which rises a legal and political superstructure and to which correspond definite forms of social consciousness . . . At a certain stage of their development, the material productive forces of society come in conflict with the existing relations of production, or — what is but a legal expression for the same thing — with the property relations within which they have been at work hitherto. From forms of development of the productive forces these relations turn into their fetters. Then begins an epoch of social revolution.[47]

At this point one important confusion must be cleared up. Historical materialism has frequently been subject to a mechanical materialist distortion in which the dialectic of forces and relations of production is interpreted simply as an antagonism between the technical instruments of production ('forces') and the system of property ownership ('relations') which operates independently of human activity, thus arriving at a theory of technological determinism. In this interpretation both Marx's key concepts undergo a reduction in their meaning. For Marx the forces of production signify not only the instruments in the sense of tools, machines etc., but the total productive capacity of society including the productive activity of the working class. 'Of all the instruments of production, the greatest productive power is the revolutionary class itself.'[48] Property ownership, on the other hand, is 'but a legal expression of relations of production.' Thus the contradiction between the forces and relations of production is not separate from the class struggle but is the very ground on which the latter arises.

This theoretical demonstration that historical materialism is history viewed from the standpoint of the proletariat is, as we have noted, more important than the question of how Marx happened to develop the theory but, in fact, its historical genesis parallels the theoretical logic almost exactly. The first comprehensive statement of historical materialism was **The German Ideology** of 1845. This work was immediately preceded by two major texts, **The Economic and Philosophic Manuscripts of 1844**, and the **Introduction to a Critique of Hegel's Philosophy of Right**. The **1844 Manuscripts** begin not with 'philosophy' or with 'alienation' but with the class struggle. The opening sentence reads: 'Wages are determined by the bitter struggle between capitalist and worker.'[49] The economic analysis that follows is, by Marx's later standards, primitive but it is carried out explicitly from the point of view of the worker. It aims to show 'from political economy itself, in its own words' that:

> . . . the worker sinks to the level of a commodity, and to a most
> miserable commodity; that the misery of the worker increases
> with the power and volume of his production; that the necessary
> result of competition is the accumulation of capital in a few

hands, and thus a restoration of monopoly in a more terrible form; and finally that the distinction between capitalist and landlord, and between agricultural labourer and industrial worker, must disappear, and the whole of society divide into the two classes of property owners and the propertyless workers.[50]

In seeking to explain this state of affairs Marx is led to an analysis of the nature of workers' labour. Workers produce the wealth of the capitalists and their own misery because their labour is alienated. Thus Marx arrives at the conception of the dual role of labour: labour as the means by which people create their life and their world, and alienated labour as the means by which they vitiate their life and create a world which stands over and against them — a dual role which implies the potential for human liberation with the abolition of alienated labour, and which thus anticipates both the starting point and conclusion of the materialist conception of history.

However, if we move back one stage further to the **Introduction to the Critique of Hegel's Philosophy of Right** (early 1844) we find already present what later appears as the result of the analysis of alienated labour and the result of historical materialism, namely the revolutionary role of the proletariat. 'When the proletariat announces the dissolution of existing social order, it only declares the secret of its own existence, for it *is* the effective dissolution of this order.'[51] And, as we have already seen, Marx's recognition of this role was itself the product of his own experience of revolutionary workers' circles in Paris. Thus both theoretically and biographically Marx's general conception of history and society can be traced back to its material basis — the proletarian struggle.

The Marxist analysis of capitalism (usually referred to as 'Marxist economics' though really it is a 'critique of political economy') was designed to provide a firm scientific foundation for the workers' movement by revealing the law of motion of the capitalist mode of production. That the entire analysis is conducted from the standpoint of the revolutionary working class should be obvious, after all its major themes include: an explanation of how workers are exploited; a demonstration that the whole system is founded on that exploitation; a prediction that *because* it is founded on exploitation this system must inevitably break down.[52] Since however this aspect of Marxism has, more than any other, been presented as 'objective', 'value-free', 'class-free', a few observations on the genesis and logic of Marx's critique of political economy seem justified.

Marx's critique is, of course, an application of the theory of historical materialism to the capitalist mode of production, and like historical materialism itself, is rooted in an analysis of *labour*[53] — an analysis of labour as alienated. It cannot be emphasised too strongly that basically Marx's theory of alienation is not a theory of how the worker 'feels' about work, or of the general state of human consciousness, but a theory of alienated *labour* — in other words of that labour which the worker is compelled to make over to another, to sell. Alienated labour *is* wage labour, not just a state of mind but 'an economic fact'.[54] However, it is also an economic fact that can only be perceived by looking at labour from the point of view of the worker. Indeed Marx was the first 'philosopher' and the first 'economist' in the history of the world to analyse the labour process from the standpoint of the worker. Just how central the theory of alienated labour is to the Marxist analysis of capitalism can be seen from two of Marx's propositions. First that 'although private property appears to be the basis and cause of alienated labour, it is rather a consequence of the latter'.[55] Second that the *differentia specifica* of capitalism is that under it labour power becomes a commodity.

A long theoretical road lies between the **1844 Manuscripts** and **Capital**, between alienated labour and the theory of surplus value. It is a road on which the early generic critique of capitalism is painstakingly transformed into a precise analytic tool with which to lay bare all the workings of the capitalist economy. But in the process the original concept is neither 'forgotten' nor 'rejected'. It remains at the heart of the analysis. Consider the following passages:

> 1) All these consequences follow from the fact that the worker is related to the product of his labour as to an alien object. For it is clear on this presupposition that the more the worker expends himself in work the more powerful becomes the world of objects which he creates in face of himself, the poorer he becomes in his inner life, and the less he belongs to himself. It is just the same as in religion. The more of himself man attributes to God, the less he has left in himself.[56]

> 2) It cannot be otherwise in a mode of production in which the

labourer exists to satisfy the needs of self-expansion of existing values, instead of, on the contrary, material wealth existing to satisfy the needs of development on the part of the labourer. As in religion man is governed by the products of his own brain, so in capitalistic production, he is governed by the products of his own hand.[57]

3) The alienation of the worker in his object is expressed as follows in the laws of political economy: the more the worker produces the less he has to consume, the more value he creates the more worthless he becomes; the more refined his product, the more crude and misshapen the worker; the more civilized the product the more barbarous the worker; the more powerful the work the more feeble the worker; the more the work manifests intelligence, the more the worker declines in intelligence and becomes a slave of nature.[58]

4) . . . within the capitalist system all methods for raising the social productiveness of labour are brought about at the cost of the individual labourer; all means for the development of production transform themselves into means of domination over, and exploitation of, the producers; they mutilate the labourer into a fragment of a man, degrade him to the level of an appendage of a machine, destroy every remnant of charm in his work and turn it into a hated toil; they estrange from him the intellectual potentialities of the labour-process in the same proportion as science is incorporated in it as one independent power; they distort the conditions under which he works, subject him during the labour-process to a despotism the more hateful for its meanness; they transform life-time into working time, and drag his wife and child beneath the wheels of the Juggernaut of capital.[59]

Passages 1) and 3) are from the **1844 Manuscripts** and 2) and 4) are from **Capital**; twenty-three years later the same basic idea, at times almost the same language. And these are only a few of numerous passages that could be quoted from all Marx's major theoretical works from **The German Ideology** to **Theories of Surplus Value**.[60]

Finally some observations on the Marxist theory of crisis, in particular its most important component, the declining rate of profit. The tendency of the rate of profit to decline is not an individual thesis, a separate proposition, which can be abstracted from the rest of Marx's thought, rather it is a point of convergence of all his major theories. It derives directly from the theory of surplus value, according to which the source of profit is the unpaid labour time of the workers, and from the proposition that under capitalism living labour falls progressively under the domination of accumulated dead labour (a theme already present in 1844). At the same time the tendency of the rate of profit to decline is the concrete economic expression of the conflict between the forces and relations of production — the proof that capitalist relations of production have become a fetter on the forces of production, that 'the real barrier of capitalist production is capital itself'.[61] Moreover, and this brings us back to our starting point, it was a theory which could only be formulated from the standpoint of the proletariat. The classical bourgeois economists observed the phenomenon of the declining rate of profit but were unable to theorise it for to do so would have been to recognise the historically limited, transitory, nature of capitalism.[62]

To some 'Marxists' it has seemed that Marx's analysis of the contradictions of capitalism is separate from his commitment to proletarian revolution. A recent proponent of this view is Lucio Colletti,[63] but the idea dates back to the Second International. Thus Rudolph Hilferding wrote that: 'It is one thing to recognise a necessity, but quite another to place oneself at the service of that necessity,'[64] with the conclusion that to get from the 'is' of capitalist breakdown to the 'ought' of socialism required a supplementary ethical commitment (usually from the 'eternal' ethical principles of Kant). Hilferding however has reversed the real logic of Marxism. It was the commitment to the proletariat that made possible the disclosure of capitalism's contradictions, and the 'ought to' of this commitment itself derived from the prior external existence of the proletariat which had already begun its struggle for self-emancipation.

To sum up the whole argument: in theory the proletarian revolution appears as the consequence of the theories of historical materialism, and surplus value etc., but in reality it is also their foundation. The empirical confirmation of this proposition is found in the fact that as a rule workers' revolutions begin spontaneously — Paris 1848 and 1871, Petrograd 1905 and 1917, Germany 1918, Spain 1936, Hungary 1956, France 1968, and so on. The role of Marxism is not to create or launch the revolution but to guide it to victory.

We are now in a position to grasp both the essential *unity* of Marxism and its developing nature — on the basis of the proletarian struggle against capital. These two great social forces, locked in battle, are continually changing and developing, as is the balance of forces between them and their interaction with other classes. Marxism must therefore change and develop too, but it must do so without departing from the standpoint of proletarian revolution. If it does so depart then it ceases to be Marxism. Lenin once described Marxism as 'a block of steel'. The metaphor is of strictly limited validity, but it is greatly preferable to the widespread view that Marxism consists of a series of detachable parts which can be discarded and replaced at will. More accurate is Lenin's contention that Marx 'laid the cornerstones of the science which socialists must advance in all directions, if they do not want to lag behind events'.[65] It is the nature of revisionism that it attempts to displace these cornerstones (which are not arbitrary but theoretical expressions of the social being of the proletariat) and in so doing departs from the standpoint of the proletariat to that of a *different class*.

Part two
The transformations of Marxism

It should already be clear that, by the criteria already established, many of the ideologists and theoretical systems that have claimed the title of Marxism in the past hundred years are not Marxist at all. Before proceeding to demonstrate this in relation to specific examples it is necessary to make some preliminary observations on the social position and consciousness of the proletariat under capitalism.

In potential the proletariat transcends capitalism, but so long as capitalism exists it remains an oppressed and exploited class. In normal times therefore the consciousness of the majority of workers is dominated by bourgeois ideology ('The ruling ideas are the ideas of the ruling class'). Yet at the same time workers are impelled by their economic position to resist the attacks of capital and to fight for improvements in their lot, even when they are not ready to challenge the system as a whole. Corresponding to this contradiction there have emerged hybrid ideologies which combine elements of bourgeois and elements of socialist ideology — the most obvious example to hand is British Labourism.

However, these hybrid ideologies also have their own distinct material base in the class whose social position is itself part bourgeois and part proletarian, namely the intermediate stratum known usually in Marxism as the petty bourgeoisie.

The category of petty bourgeois has a general validity, but it must not be allowed to obscure the fact that in the modern world it covers a number of social layers whose conditions of existence are markedly different. The most important of these are: the 'old' petty bourgeoisie of small shopkeepers and other small employers; the 'new' middle class of salaried employees in positions of authority over the working class; the trade union and labour movement bureaucracy; and in most countries, the peasantry. Taken together these groups 'surround' the proletariat (they are in much closer daily contact with it than is the bourgeoisie) and exert an influence on its consciousness. Each of the groups, however, tends to generate its own version of petty bourgeois ideology and to exert its own kind of pressure on the workers. The consciousness of the proletariat, and with it Marxist theory, exists therefore in a permanent state of siege and the history of Marxism has been a history of battles with the hybrid ideologies of the petty bourgeoisie: hence Marx's polemics against Proudhon and Bakunin, Engels' against Dühring, Plekhanov and Lenin against the Narodniks, and so on.

The problem which concerns this article however is conflicts within 'Marxism', or rather between theoretical and political tendencies that *claim* to be Marxist. The question that must be posed is whether the most important of these conflicts are also struggles between the standpoint of the proletariat and that of the petty bourgeoisie or other alien classes. If this is a phenomenon that can be established it also needs to be explained. Lenin suggested that 'The dialectics of history is such that the theoretical victory of Marxism forces its enemies to *disguise themselves* as Marxists.'[66] But although this explanation contains an important kernel of truth it is somewhat over-conspiratorial. It is more historically accurate to suggest that the process usually runs on these lines: leaders or movements arrive at a perspective of proletarian revolution and adopt Marxism, then for a variety of reasons (in the last analysis the pressure of capitalism) they move away from this perspective but retain the label and language of Marxism — either through self-deception or a desire to preserve their radical credentials or both — while transforming its real content. Once this process has occurred this 'transformed' Marxism can be passed on to other leaders and movements that have never had anything to do with proletarian revolution.[67] But this is to anticipate results that have first to be demonstrated by historical analysis.

The history of Marxism since Marx has been dominated, in terms of material power and numbers of adherents, by three tendencies: firstly, the social democracy of the Second International; secondly Stalinism; and thirdly, Third World nationalism. Clearly it is out of the question to present, within the confines of this small book, a comprehensive analysis of any one, let alone all three, of these tendencies. I shall therefore approach each in terms of the most important features of its most important representatives.

1
Kautskyism

The leading party of the Second International was German Social Democracy, the SPD. Founded in 1875 at the Gotha Conference, which united Marx's German supporters with the followers of Lassalle,[68] the party developed through a period of semi-legality (Bismarck's anti-socialist laws) into a position, by the turn of the century, of considerable strength within the German state. This was a period of general advance for German capitalism within which it was possible for the developing working-class movement to win concessions and improvements in its lot. Of course these gains were the result of struggle — capitalism never gives anything without some fight — but they required no overall confrontation, no life or death class battle. (In fact the level of strikes in Germany was very low.[69]) As a whole it was a time of relative social peace and the German working class took advantage of this to build the largest, best organised socialist party in the world — a party with hundreds of thousands of members, thousands of party organisations, and over eighty daily papers, as well as a multitude of social and cultural organisations.

From the late 1890s this party was divided into an 'orthodox Marxist' majority and a (growing) 'revisionist' minority. The latter, led by Eduard Bernstein, maintained that capitalism, contrary to Marxist theory, was gradually overcoming its contradictions and that therefore the SPD could and should be no more than a party of democratic social reform. Since the revisionists were more or less openly anti-Marxist they are not essentially relevant to this article: it is the 'orthodox' wing that concerns us here.

The SPD officially committed itself to Marxism at its congress at Erfurt in 1891 when it adopted the Erfurt Programme drafted by the 'Pope of Marxism', Karl Kautsky. This programme, together with the commentary on it, also by Kautsky,[70] remained the basic statement of the movement's world outlook, just as Kautsky remained its leading theorist, until the First World War. Without doubt the Erfurt Programme was intended, and generally accepted, as a statement of completely orthodox Marxism. Its first section is 'an analysis of present day society and its development',[71] and consists of a condensed and simplified exposition of the theory of capitalist development outlined by Marx in **The Communist Manifesto** culminating in the proposition that 'private ownership of the means of production has become irreconcilable with their effective use and complete development'.[72] Its second section calls for the resolution of this contradiction by 'the conversion of private ownership into social ownership and conversion of commodity production into socialist production carried on for and by society'.[73] The third section deals with 'the means which are to lead to the realisation of these objects',[74] namely the class struggle of the proletariat. With regard to the nature of this struggle the programme tells us:

> The struggle of the working class against capitalist exploitation is necessarily a political struggle. The working class cannot develop its economic organisation and wage its economic battles without political rights. It cannot accomplish the transfer of the means of production to the community as a whole without first having come into possession of political power.[75]

We are here still on the grounds of orthodoxy. Time and again Marx insisted that 'the struggle of class against class is a political struggle', that 'to conquer power had therefore become the great duty of the working classes'.[76] But what was to be the content of this 'political struggle', this 'conquest of political power'? For Marx, as we have seen, it was above all the destruction of the bourgeois state and the establishment of the dictatorship of the proletariat — the concrete example of which was the Paris Commune. What it was for Kautsky and the SPD is shown clearly in Kautsky's commentary on the programme — namely an exclusively *parliamentary* struggle. To demonstrate just how exclusively parliamentarist the SPD strategy was, a lengthy quotation is unfortunately necessary:

> Like every other class, the working class must strive to influence the state authorities, to bend them to its purposes.
>
> Great capitalists can influence rulers and legislators directly, but the workers can do so *only through parliamentary activity* [my emphasis throughout] . . . By electing representatives to parliament therefore the working class can exercise an influence over the governmental powers.
>
> The struggle of all the classes which depend upon legislative action for political influence is directed, in the modern state, on the one hand toward an increase in the power of the parliament (or congress), and on the other toward an increase in their own influence within the parliament. The power of parliament depends on the energy and courage of the classes behind it and on the energy and courage of the classes on which its will is to be imposed. The influence of a class within a parliament depends, in the first place, on the nature of the electoral law in force. It is dependent further on the influence of the class in question among the voters, and, lastly, upon its aptitude for parliamentary work . . .
>
> The proletariat is, however . . . favourably situated in regard to parliamentary activity . . . Their unions are to them an excellent parliamentary school; they afford opportunities in training in parliamentary law and public speaking . . . Moreover it finds in its own ranks an increasing number of persons well fitted to represent it in legislative halls.
>
> Whenever the proletariat engages in parliamentary activity as a self-conscious class, parliamentarism begins to change its character. *It ceases to be a mere tool in the hands of the bourgeoisie.* This very participation of the proletariat proves to be the most effective means of shaking up the hitherto indifferent divisions of the proletariat and giving them hope and confidence. *It is the most powerful level that can be utilised* to raise the proletariat out of its economic, social and moral degradation.
>
> *The proletariat has, therefore, no reason to distrust parliamentary action.*[77]

This parliamentary perspective was adopted in response

to the dramatic electoral gains of the SPD — its vote rose from 550,000 (9.7 per cent) in 1884 to 1,427,000 (19.7 per cent) in 1890 — and it constituted a definite shift to the right from earlier positions. In 1881 Kautsky had written that, 'Social Democracy harbours no illusions that it can directly achieve its goal through elections, through the parliamentary road' and that 'the first step of the coming revolution' would be to 'demolish the bourgeois state'.[78] But from the 1890s onwards the parliamentary road remained the dominant strategy of both Kautsky and the SPD. Thus, when in the controversies with the revisionists within his own party, Kautsky appears as the defender of 'revolution' it is a conception of 'parliamentary revolution' that he is defending: in other words that the workers' party will remain in opposition, refusing all coalitions or participation in bourgeois governments until such time as it has won an overall majority in parliament and forms the government, whereupon it will use its position to legislate the introduction to socialism.[79] That this strategy involved taking over, not smashing, the capitalist state was emphasised by Kautsky himself in his 1912 polemic against Pannekoek:

> The objective of our political struggle remains what it has been up to now: the conquest of state power through the conquest of a majority in parliament and the elevation of parliament to a commanding position within the state. Certainly not the destruction of state power.[80]

Underpinning the parliamentary strategy was a view of the transition to socialism as the more or less inevitable outcome of economic development. The growth of capitalism would mean the growth of the proletariat. As the proletariat grew so its consciousness would rise and that would mean more votes for Social Democracy, until such time as there would be an overwhelming majority for socialism. 'Economic development', wrote Kautsky, 'will lead naturally to the accomplishment of this purpose.'[81] The whole process would go ahead smoothly, inevitably, and without any life or death struggles, provided only that the party leadership did not fall into adventurism and provoke premature battle. The only actual activity required was organisation and education:

> Building up the organisation, winning all positions of power,

which we are able to win and hold securely by our own strength, studying the state and society and educating the masses: other aims we cannot consciously and systematically set either to ourselves or to our organisations.[82]

The question we must now pose, following the methodology adopted in the first part of this article, is: what was the social basis of this ideology of passive expectancy? In one sense, clearly, the social base was the period of detente between the proletariat and the bourgeoisie which accompanied the prosperity and advance of German capital at the end of the nineteenth and beginning of the twentieth century. At the same time, however, within this general situation this ideology expressed the interests, not of the working class, but of the social layer whose very existence was a product of this social truce: namely the vast Social Democratic and trade union bureaucracy, the army of privileged officials, who had arisen to administer their beloved organisations.

Nothing illustrates this better than the attitude of these trade union and party leaders to that fundamental question of the class struggle, the mass strike — a question that became urgent in Germany as a result of the role of the mass strike in the Russian Revolution of 1905.[83] The trade union leaders were implacably opposed to the mass strike and, at the Cologne Congress of the trade unions in May 1905, adopted a resolution condemning it. The party, however, at Jena in September 1905, passed a resolution 'accepting' the mass strike in principle without specifying what should be done about it. Then the outbreak of a mass movement in Saxony for the widening of the franchise demanded the resolution of this contradiction in practice:

> On 1 February 1906 a secret conference of executives of the party and the unions was held. This gathering promptly revealed the real balance of forces between the two organisations. The party capitulated to the unions, committing itself to trying to prevent a mass strike with all its might.[84]

This was followed by a compromise at the Mannheim Party Congress in September 1906, where the unions and the party reached agreement on the basis of 'common theoretical acceptance of the possibility of recourse to the mass strike in the indeterminate future', and then only with 'the adherence of the leaders and the members of the unions.'[85] Kautsky's role in this process was that of a 'left' critic of the union leaders. He complained of their narrow economistic outlook and called for the supremacy of the Social Democratic spirit in the unions, but he *refused to break with them* and simultaneously attacked the real advocates of the mass strike (such as Rosa Luxemburg) as 'fabricators of revolution'.[86] When faced with a choice Kautsky sacrificed the demands of the class struggle to the unity of the party and trade union organisations.

The labour movement bureaucracy is part of the petty bourgeoisie. It stands between labour and capital and its objective role is that of mediator between the classes. In relation to the mass of workers it is privileged in terms of income, job security, working conditions and life style. However its position, and consequently its political behaviour, is different from that of the traditional petty-bourgeoisie of small businessmen, shopkeepers, self-employed, and so on. The latter, as owners of private property, are in normal times more or less completely under the hegemony of the big bourgeoisie. In times of crisis, when they are squeezed between labour and capital, they can be pulled behind the working class by a powerful revolutionary movement that shows its determination and capacity to resolve the crisis of capitalism. In the absence of such a movement they can swing far to the right and form the mass base of fascism.

By contrast the labour bureaucracy is organisationally bound to the working class and therefore, as a social layer, cannot swing so far to the right (which is why the theory of 'social fascism' is such nonsense). At the same time however it has a much closer relationship to the ruling class than does the small employer. Its role as 'representative' (parliamentary or union) brings it into daily contact with the bosses and their state, and it depends for its mass support on the concessions it can obtain from them. Threatened equally by fascism, which would destroy its 'organisations', and revolution, which would destroy its negotiating role, it is profoundly conservative. It fears, above all, mass actions that might 'get out of hand', disrupt the organisations, provoke a ruling class offensive, and undermine its delicate balancing act between the classes. Its political need is for an ideology that combines socialism in words with passivity and compromise in deeds. It needs the working class to sustain the organisations that pay its salaries, and as a stage army that can be wheeled into battle to gain concessions which in turn retain support for the organisations, but it needs the working class in its place and under control. The ideology of German Social Democracy fitted these needs like a glove. Kautsky's 'Marxism' was a theoretical system that in all crucial questions adapted itself to the needs of the bureaucracy.

This was true even at the level of philosophy. For mechanical materialism, the philosophical outlook characteristic of Kautsky and the Second International as a whole, is, as we have shown, a bourgeois position at bottom. It treats the working class as a merely passive product of material circumstances, and therefore excludes the active revolutionary role of the workers, and particularly of the party.[87]

Once this social basis of Second International Marxism has been grasped (and what was true for Kautsky and the SPD was even more true for most of the other socialist parties), the capitulation to chauvinism in the First World War presents no particular problems of analysis. On the one hand the various bureaucracies had developed a vested interest in the prosperity and imperial power of their respective national capitals — the greater that prosperity the more easily they could negotiate concessions. On the other hand they could not risk an unpopular stand that would jeopardise their legality, their organisations, and their support. Thus on 4 August 1914, the SPD's vote for war credits was a betrayal — of all the fine anti-war and internationalist rhetoric of the previous years — but it was also the continuation and culmination of well-established political practice.[88]

In conclusion, to describe Kautskyism as a variant of Marxism, or as one aspect of the Marxist tradition, is to mistake form for content. In content it was the theory of a different class. In content the anti-Marxist Bernstein and the 'orthodox' Marxist Kautsky stood much closer to each other than either did to the revolutionary theory of Marx. They differed not on what political practice should be but on how it should be described. We will leave the last word to Kautsky himself. In his 1932 obituary of Bernstein he wrote that their polemics at the turn of the century were 'only an episode', that they had come together 'during the World War' and that subsequently on all questions, of war, of revolution, of the evolution of Germany and of the world, 'we have always adopted the same point of view.'[89]

2
Stalinism

Stalinism's point of departure was very different from that of Kautskyism. Stalinism emerged within the Bolshevik Party in the years following the Civil War and rose to dominance in the Soviet Union through a series of bitter inner party struggles in the 1920s, finally achieving absolute control in 1928–29. Theoretically, therefore, it evolved out of Leninism, the development of Marxism which expressed and guided to victory the workers' revolution of October 1917. Leninism's principal characteristics were its revolutionary intransigence, its fierce internationalism, its analysis of and opposition to imperialism, its insistence on the destruction of the bourgeois state by workers' power based on soviets, and its conception of the party as an interventionist vanguard organisation.

However, the material situation in which Stalinism was born was almost the opposite of that expressed in its theoretical starting point. The Russian working class, which in 1917 had reached the highest level of consciousness and revolutionary struggle yet seen anywhere in the world, had, by 1921, virtually ceased to exist. In the course of the Civil War the vast majority of the most militant and politically conscious workers had either been killed in battle or raised to the position of state officials. Under the combined impact of the Civil War, the Revolution itself, and the World War that preceded it the Russian economy had collapsed utterly. Gross industrial production fell to 31 per cent of its 1913 level, large scale industrial production to 21 per cent, production of steel to 4.7 per cent, the transport system was in ruins, epidemics and famine raged. The total of industrial workers fell from about three million in 1917 to one and a quarter million in 1921, and those that remained were politically exhausted. As Lenin put it in 1921:

> [The] industrial proletariat . . . in our country, owing to the war and to the desperate poverty and ruin has become declassed, i.e. dislodged from its class groove and has ceased to exist as a proletariat.[90]

The Bolshevik party found itself suspended in a vacuum. To administer the country it had to take over and use a vast army of Tsarist officials and against all its intentions it itself became bureaucratised. Bureaucracy is essentially a hierarchy of officials not subject to popular control from below. In Russia the social force that Marxists (above all Lenin) counted on to prevent the development of bureaucracy, an active revolutionary working class, had been cut from under the feet of the party. In this situation it was impossible to implement the Marxist programme in pure form. For a period it was possible to mount a holding operation, relying on the hardened socialist commitment of the Bolshevik old guard, to cling to the basic revolutionary aspirations while making the necessary practical compromises (for example the New Economic Policy or NEP) and waiting for help from the international revolution. This in essence was the course taken by Lenin. But failing the international revolution (and it did fail) a stark choice had eventually to be made. Either remain loyal to the theory and goal of international proletarian revolution, with the possibility of losing state power in Russia, or cling to power and abandon the theory and goal. The situation was extremely complex and the participants did not see it in these clear terms, but, essentially, Trotskyism was the product of the first choice and Stalinism of the second.[91]

But of course Stalinism did not ditch Leninism or Marxism openly. In order to retain the aura and prestige of Leninism, Stalinism had to perform two interconnected operations.

First the transformation of Marxism-Leninism from a developing practice-oriented doctrine into a fixed dogma, the equivalent of a state religion, was necessary. Stalin's aspiration in this direction appears clearly in his 'Oath to Lenin' delivered shortly after Lenin's death:

> In leaving us, Comrade Lenin ordained us to hold high and keep pure the great title of member of the party. We vow to thee, Comrade Lenin, that we shall honourably fulfil this thy commandment . . . In leaving us, Comrade Lenin ordained us to guard the unity of our party like the apple of our eye. We vow to thee Comrade Lenin that we shall fulfil honourably this thy commandment, too . . . In leaving us, Comrade Lenin ordained us to guard and strengthen the dictatorship of the proletariat. We vow to thee Comrade Lenin, that without sparing our strength we shall honourably fulfil this thy commandment too . . .[92]

Also expressions of this tendency were Stalin's **Foundations of Leninism** — a rigid schematic codification of Lenin's principles — and the vast mass of self-styled Marxist texts and formal Soviet academic commentaries that continue to pour from the party's publishing houses to this day. In this form Stalinist Marxism was completely severed from the practice of the working class and thus became completely lifeless. (It is anything but an accident that, oppositionists apart, not a single Marxist thinker of any stature has emerged from Stalinist or post-Stalinist Russia.) No longer concerned with changing reality, its function was to mask it. Stalinist Marxism became ideology in the fullest sense of the word.

If for this purpose Stalin would have liked to preserve Leninism untouched, embalmed like Lenin's body in the mausoleum, he was nonetheless unable to. The gap between theory and reality became so wide that 'certain amendments' to the theory were unavoidable if even the appearance of their correspondence was to be maintained.[93] Thus a second operation — the revision of Leninism and Marxism to bring it into line with actual Stalinist practice — arose as a necessary consequence of the first. It is by focussing on this process that we can gain the clearest insight into the real structure of Stalinist Marxism and the interests it represented.

By far the most important such amendment was the theory of socialism in one country, first promulgated by Stalin in autumn 1924. The introduction of this theory needs to be considered from a number of angles: how it was done, why it was done, the social interests it served, and its consequences.

First Stalin's method. 'Socialism in one country' marked a dramatic break with the internationalist position formulated by Marx and Engels as early as 1845 and 1847[94] and tirelessly repeated by Lenin in relation to the Russian Revolution.[95] It also contradicted what Stalin himself had written in **The Foundation of Leninism** as late as April 1924:

> The main task of socialism — the organisation of socialist production — still remains ahead. Can this task be accomplished, can the final victory of socialism in one country be attained without the joint efforts of the proletariat of several advanced countries? No, this is impossible.[96]

Stalin 'solved' this contradiction by rewriting this passage to read the opposite ('After consolidating its power and leading the peasantry in its wake the proletariat of the victorious country can and must build a socialist society'[97]) and having the first edition withdrawn from circulation. There was no new analysis, simply the assertion of a new orthodoxy (retrospectively grafted on to Lenin). Indeed, apart from this one passage the rest of the text was left unchanged, including passages which clearly reflected the earlier perspective.[98] Only later were 'analyses' concocted to justify the new line.

This procedure was not an isolated example, rather it was typical. When Social Democracy (according to Stalin) changed from an ally (1925–27) to 'the main enemy' (1928–33) and then back to an ally again (1934–39), the change of line was not based on any new analysis of Social Democracy. It was simply a *fiat* to which analysis had to accommodate itself afterwards. The 'secret' of this method is not that Stalin had *no* analysis but that the analysis he had could not be spoken publicly, because its real criteria, and real purposes, had ceased to be those of the theory whose language it retained.

What then was Stalin's reason for introducing socialism in one country in 1924? Clearly it was a response (a defeatist response) to the failure of the German Revolution in 1923 and the relative stabilisation of capitalism that followed. Stalin had never been much interested in world revolution (he was by far the most insular of the leading Bolsheviks) and now he wrote it off entirely, but this alone does not explain why he didn't simply continue to pay lip service to the old internationalism. The answer is that socialism in one country fitted exactly the needs and aspirations of the bureaucrats now dominating the country. They longed for business as usual, uncomplicated by international revolutionary adventures. At the same time, they needed a banner around which to group themselves, a slogan defining their goal. As Trotsky put it, socialism in one country 'expressed unmistakeably the mood of the bureaucracy. When speaking of the victory of socialism, they meant their own victory.'[99] It was to the bureaucracy what 'All power to the soviets' was to the working class in 1917.

As we have seen, Stalin introduced his new theory with the minimum of fuss (precisely to disguise its newness) yet in reality it marked a decisive shift in orientation which had the most far-reaching consequences. The Soviet Union was isolated in the face of a hostile capitalist world — a world which had already demonstrated its eagerness to strangle the Revolution by its intervention in the Civil War, and which, as Lenin emphasised, remained economically and militarily stronger than the young workers' state. The strategy of the early years of the Revolution — the strategy of Lenin and Trotsky — included, of course, the most determined military defence but ultimately it relied on stimulating international revolution to overthrow capitalism from within. The policy of socialism in one country changed this emphasis. It replaced reliance on the international class struggle with reliance on the power of the Soviet Union as a nation state, and this decision had its own implacable logic.

The defence of the Soviet state demanded armed forces equal to those of its enemies and in the modern world that meant an equivalent industry and an equivalent surplus. Engels had already grasped this crucial fact of 20th century economics and politics in 1892:

> From the moment warfare became part of the *grande industrie* (iron clad ships, rifled artillery, quickfiring and repeating cannons, repeating rifles, steel covered bullets, smokeless powder etc.) *la grande industrie*, without which all these things cannot be made, became a political necessity. All these things cannot be had without a highly developed metal manufacture. And that manufacture cannot be had without a corresponding development in all other branches of manufacture, especially textiles.[100]

Stalin's grasp on this reality was no less firm:

No comrades . . . the pace must not be slackened! On the contrary, we must quicken it as much as is within our powers and possibilities.

To slacken the pace would mean to lag behind; and those who lag behind are beaten. We do not want to be beaten. No, we don't want to. The history of old . . . Russia . . . she was ceaselessly beaten for her backwardness . . . For military backwardness, for cultural backwardness, for political backwardness, for industrial backwardness, for agricultural backwardness . . . We are fifty or a hundred years behind the advanced countries. We must make good this lag in ten years. Either we do it or they crush us.

But Russia was poor, compared with its rivals desperately so, and its productivity of labour was low. To industrialise it required massive investment and without international aid there was only one possible source for this investment, the labour of its workers and peasants. A massive surplus had to be extracted and ploughed back into industrial growth. But with the majority of the population living not much above subsistence level there was no way such a surplus could be extracted and set aside voluntarily by collective decision of the associated producers. It could be done only through forcible exploitation and that in turn required an agency to apply this force — a social class freed from the burdens, but reaping the benefits, of the process of capital accumulation — a class playing the same historical role as the bourgeoisie had done in western Europe. Thus the consequence, in practice, of socialism in one country was its direct opposite, state capitalism in one country.

Socialism in one country also had theoretical consequences. It could not be confined, much as Stalin may have wished it, to a minor amendment to the orthodoxy. In Russia the overwhelming majority of the population were not workers but peasants. Marx and Lenin, although they recognised the possibility of a revolutionary alliance between workers and peasants to overthrow the capitalists and landlords, always insisted that the peasantry was not a socialist class. 'The peasant movement . . . is not a struggle against the foundations of capitalism but a struggle to cleanse them of all survivals of serfdom.'[102] But if Russia, by itself, was to accomplish the transition to socialism, then this attitude to the peasantry had to be revised. So for a period Stalin (and his ally Bukharin) advanced the notion of the peasantry 'growing into' socialism. In practice of course the peasantry was crushed by the forced collectivisation of 1929–33, for it constituted an obstacle not only to socialism but also to state capitalism, but not before the blurring of the distinction between the working class and the peasantry had passed into Stalinist ideology.

Another casualty was the theory of imperialism. This had been developed by Luxemburg, Bukharin and Lenin as an analysis of the latest stage of world capitalism and it asserted, above all, the primacy of the world economy over all its constituent national parts. Socialism in one country necessarily denied this. Indeed, in seeking to defend his theory against the objections of the Left Opposition, who pointed out that Marx and Engels had explicitly rejected 'national' socialism, Stalin was led to argue that while socialism in one country was impossible under the industrial capitalism of Marx's day, it *was* possible under imperialism which was characterised by the 'law of uneven development'.[103] In this way Stalinism deprived the Leninist theory of imperialism of its real analytical content and reduced it to mere anti-colonialism, not at all a distinctively Marxist position.

Finally the logic of socialism in one country played havoc with the Marxist theory of the state. By 1934 Stalin was claiming that socialism had been established in Russia. This was on the basis that with the transformation of the peasantry into state employees, classes no longer existed — the bureaucracy of course was not a class for Stalin. According to Marxism, the state, as an instrument of class rule, was destined to wither away under socialism, but Stalin's state had not the slightest intention of withering away, and this was a fact that no amount of propaganda could hide.

Stalin fielded this particular contradiction by asserting that Marx and Engels had expected the state to wither away because they viewed socialism as an international phenomenon, whereas when socialism existed only in one country the state had to be strengthened.[104] It was the kind of circular argument that works well when anyone who points out the circularity is a candidate for the firing squad.

But if this argument justified the existence of the state it still left unsolved the problem of the class nature of this state. It could not be a specifically workers' state if Russia was a classless society — and precisely this was involved in the claim that Russia was socialist. The only solution was the notion that the Soviet state had become a state of 'the whole people', a thoroughly bourgeois view of the state vigorously attacked by Marx in his **Critique of the Gotha Programme** and by Lenin in **The State and Revolution**. Moreover it was a view of the state adopted by the Stalinist bureaucracy for exactly the same reason that the bourgeoisie has always viewed their state as a state of the whole people, namely its refusal to acknowledge its own existence as a ruling class.

It is useful at this point to note the ideological similarities and differences between Stalinism and Kautskyism. Both involved a systematic separation of theory and practice, in contrast to the Marxist aim of the unity of theory and practice. Both evinced a strong attachment to the state in contrast to the sharp hostility of Marx and Lenin. Both collapsed from internationalism to nationalism. Yet the differences are equally striking. Kautskyism blunted Marxism in theory and then further blunted it in practice; it spoke of social revolution (through parliament) and practised conciliation with the bourgeoisie. Stalinism retained a more revolutionary rhetoric and practised the complete opposite: it spoke of insurrection and the dictatorship of the proletariat and practised the outright suppression of the working class. Kautskyism was awed and attracted by the power of the state and therefore unwilling to contemplate its destruction. Stalinism developed a positive cult of state worship. Whereas for Marx and Lenin the dictatorship of the proletariat was already a 'semi-state' or 'no longer a state in the proper sense of the word',[105] for Stalinism the road to socialism (and even communism) lay through strengthening the state *ad infinitum*. Kautskyism capitulated to nationalism in 1914 shamefacedly and under the cover of 'peace' slogans. Stalinism, having formally inserted nationalism into Marxism with 'socialism in one country', degenerated into the crudest possible Great Russian chauvinism, even exalting Russia's Tsarist imperialist past.[106]

These similarities and differences reflected similarities and differences in the social bases of the two ideologies. Both were ideologies of bureaucracies that had risen from the working class movement, but in the case of Kautskyism the bureaucracy stood midway between the proletariat and the bourgeoisie, whereas the Stalinist bureaucracy, with the old bourgeoisie annihilated and effectively declassed, actually found itself in power. Kautskyism consequently appeared as a moderate, cautious 'Marxism' which pushed to the fore the elements of Marxism 'acceptable to the bourgeoisie'.[107] Whereas Stalinism appeared as an arrogant, ruthless 'Marxism' with little or no regard for the feelings of the bourgeoisie but which transformed the content of this theory into its extreme opposite. However, just as Kautskyism had more in common with its opponent Bernstein than it did with Marxism, so, at bottom, Stalinism, for all its verbal denunciations, stood far closer to Kautskyism than it did to the revolutionary theory of Marx and Lenin.

The parallels with Social Democracy become even clearer once we examine Stalinism as an international phenomenon. So far the focus of our attention has been on Stalinism within Russia but it also had a major impact beyond Russia's borders, first and foremost through the parties of the Communist International (the Comintern), all of which rapidly absorbed the Stalinist world outlook. This impact itself needs a note of explanation.

From the outset the Comintern was dominated by its Russian section; as was only to be expected given that they were its founders and had the authority of the successful Revolution behind them. But in the early years there was full and free debate and western Communist leaders felt able to challenge the Russians even if the latter's point of view generally prevailed. However, the defeat of the European revolutionary wave between 1919 and 1923 undermined the confidence of the western parties and emphasised their sense of inferiority to the seemingly victorious Russians. This, combined with the increased use of bureaucratic pressure and material aid, confirmed and intensified Russian domination of the Comintern to the point where it could be used to divert the International fundamentally from its original purpose of world proletarian revolution.

The ideological medium through which this shift was effected was again the theory of socialism in one country. If the main task, the establishment of socialism, could be achieved in one country, then the international revolution became a kind of optional extra or bonus, a distant goal to be rendered occasional homage, rather than an immediate necessity guiding practical activity. One consequence of this was the establishment of a tendency to reduce the role of the Communist Parties to 'frontier patrols' for the Soviet state. Their first duty was to hinder any possibility of military intervention against Russia and to this end they were induced to act as reformist pressure groups on their respective bourgeoisies, downplaying revolutionary politics for fear of alienating potential friends and allies.

The first fruits of this orientation were the subordination of the Chinese Communist Party to the 'progressive' bourgeois nationalist Kuomintang, which resulted in the smashing of the Chinese Revolution of 1925–27 by that same Kuomintang; and the subordination of the British Communist Party to the 'left' leaders of the TUC General Council, who were simultaneously posing as 'friends of the Soviet Union' in the Anglo-Soviet Trade Union Committee and betraying the General Strike of 1926. Later fruits included the Popular Fronts of the mid-1930s, with their sacrifice of the Spanish Revolution (and therefore the Spanish Republic) to Franco, for the sake of a potential Soviet alliance with bourgeois democratic Britain and France, and, eventually, the dissolution of the Comintern itself in 1943, as a gesture of good will to the Allies in the Second World War.

However, if the parties of the Comintern were to be manipulated in this way they had to be transformed organisationally as well as ideologically. The mass of members of the Communist Parties were, undoubtedly, sincere workers who had joined their parties in order to overthrow capitalism. If they accepted the theory of socialism in one country it was precisely because they did not understand its implications. Moreover, their class position would continually impel them to act in ways that transcended the role of Soviet frontier patrols. Consequently to impose this role on them, the parties of the Comintern had to be removed from the control of their members — they had to be bureaucratised, staffed by a hierarchy of officials who could be relied upon to subordinate the interests of the working class (and of their own worker members) to the interests of the ruling bureaucracy in Russia. With the power, prestige and funds available to it Stalinism did not find this a difficult task. By the end of the 1920s the Comintern and its parties were entirely in the hands of thoroughly 'reliable' Stalinist *apparatchiks*.

Yet it must also be understood that there was an inherent limit to this process. If the Comintern parties were to be *effective* frontier patrols, more effective than the Soviet diplomatic corps, then they had to dispose of certain forces, they had to have mass support, and for historical reasons that support would be predominantly working class. To gain and retain that support they would have to be, to a certain extent, responsive to the needs of that class. Thus, just as the Social Democratic bureaucracy mediates between the proletariat and the bourgeoisie to the advantage of the latter, so the bureaucracies of the Communist Parties mediated between the interests of their local proletariat and the interests of Russian state capitalism, also to the advantage of the latter.

At the same time, however, socialism in one country generated a second, and contradictory, tendency within international communism. Since it was a nationalist theory as applied to Russia, it opened the doors to nationalism within every Communist Party. As Trotsky put it at the time:

> If it is at all possible to realise socialism in one country, then one can believe in that theory not only *after* but *before* the conquest of power. If socialism can be realised within the national boundaries of backward Russia, then there is all the more reason to believe that it can be realised in advanced Germany . . . It will be the beginning of the disintegration of the Comintern along the lines of social-patriotism.[108]

At first this nationalist tendency lay dormant, overshadowed by loyalty to Russia. But the very process of working as Soviet frontier patrols, of building bridges to the nationalist bourgeoisie in the backward countries (China) or the reformist trade union leaders (Britain) or the 'democratic' bourgeoisie (the Popular Fronts in Spain and France) itself fostered the nationalist infection. That the nationalist tendency remained subordinate to the frontier patrol tendency up until the Second World War was shown by the general Comintern acceptance of the Soviet line that the war was an imperialist war (a line dictated by Stalin's temporary alliance with Hitler). The nationalist tendency then received a massive boost from the Soviet switch in 1941 (induced by the German invasion of Russia) to the line that the war was now an anti-fascist people's war, which demanded the complete cessation of independent working-class struggle and required Communists to act as super-patriots.

After the war the nationalist tendency grew apace. In those countries where Communist Parties came to power by their own efforts (China, Yugoslavia, Albania) it triumphed completely and led to open breaks with Moscow. It remained weakest in those parties installed in power by the Red Army (Poland, Hungary, East Germany among others) and in parties that were small, persecuted or exiled and thus dependent on Soviet patronage (for example the Greek and the Portuguese). It became dominant in parties with a mass working-class base which aspired to a role in government (most notably the Italian).[109] The phenomenon of Eurocommunism was the ideological reflection of this process.

Set aside for the moment the question of Stalinism in the under-developed countries and consider the elements we have traced in the evolution of western Stalinism: reformist pressure group politics, dependence on trade union leaders, alliances with the 'left' of the bourgeoisie, nationalism and bureaucratic organisations. What is this but a carbon copy of the elements that made up Social Democracy? Small wonder then that the ideological positions of western Stalinism — national parliamentary roads to socialism, explicit rejection of the dictatorship of the proletariat, and so on — have become increasingly indistinguishable from those of Social Democracy. The parallel extends even to the division of Left and Right Eurocommunism. Left Eurocommunism is more or less a return to Kautskyism in that it envisages a more or less rapid parliamentary transition to socialism, backed by mass pressure of course.[110] Right Eurocommunism is more or less equivalent to Bernsteinism in that it envisages nothing more radical than coalitions (the Italian 'historic compromise') and thus is to the right of traditional Social Democracy's left wing. (Compare the current positions of the 'Marxist' Eric Hobsbawm and the 'non-Marxist' Tony Benn in Britain).

To conclude: Stalinist 'Marxism' has taken two forms. The first, in Russia, was the ideology of the counter-revolutionary bureaucracy which established itself, in the name of socialism, as a state capitalist ruling class. The second, principally in Europe, has evolved from being the ideology of bureaucratic agents of the first into the ideology of a section of the labour movement bureaucracy in its own right. These two forms are different and cannot simply be equated — but on the fundamental question, the international workers' revolution, the self-emancipation of the world working class, they are united in their opposition. Neither is in any sense part of the genuine Marxist tradition.

In the third world, Stalinist 'Marxism' has evolved somewhat differently.

3
Third world nationalism

The first Marxist to recognise the significance of third world national liberation movements was Lenin. His analysis of imperialism demonstrated the 'colonial and financial enslavement of the vast majority of the world's population by an insignificant minority of the richest and advanced capitalist countries'[111] and showed that this enslavement would inevitably provoke a wave of revolts and wars of liberation. What Lenin envisaged was a world alliance between the proletarian revolution, principally in the west, and the national liberation movements, principally in the east, to crush imperialism in a pincer movement. He insisted therefore that it was of the utmost importance for Communists to support these nationalist movements, especially in struggles against their 'own' imperialism.

At the same time Lenin realised that this strategy carried with it the danger of blurring the Marxist distinction 'between the interests of the oppressed classes, of working and exploited people and the general concept of national interests as a whole, which implies the interests of the ruling class'.[112] Lenin's theses on this question at the Second Congress of the Comintern, therefore, stressed the following:

> . . . the need for a determined struggle against attempts to give a communist colouring to bourgeois-democratic liberation trends in the backward countries . . . The Communist International

must enter into a temporary alliance with bourgeois democracy in the colonial and backward countries, but should not merge with it, and should under all circumstances uphold the independence of the proletarian movement even if it is in its most embryonic form.[113]

Lenin also warned against 'the deception systematically practised by the imperialist powers' of setting up states which were formally politically independent, but economically and militarily wholly dependent. His conclusion was that:

Under present-day international conditions there is no salvation for dependent and weak nations except in a union of Soviet republics . . . Complete victory over capitalism cannot be won unless the proletariat, and following it, the mass of working people in all countries and nations throughout the world voluntarily strive for alliance and unity.[114]

Under Stalin, however, the policy of the Comintern, dictated by the need to win friends for the Soviet Union, proceeded in precisely the direction warned against by Lenin. The classic case, of course, was China, where the Chinese Communist Party not only entered the bourgeois nationalist Kuomintang party, but also accepted a prohibition on criticising the principles of Sun Yat-sen, its founder, and handed its own membership list over to the Kuomintang leadership. Chiang Kai-shek was made an honorary member of the Communist International.

The process of giving bourgeois nationalist movements a 'communist colouring' and merging Communism with bourgeois nationalism received a further intensification after the Second World War, when selective support for national liberation movements in the opposing camp became an important element in the Soviet Union's global power struggle with the United States.[115] By the 1950s and 1960s a situation had been reached where, on the one hand, almost every nationalist regime and movement in the third world called itself 'socialist' and many claimed to be 'Marxist', while on the other hand large sections of the left in the advanced countries, including the non-Stalinist left and including some of Trotskyist lineage, had come to regard the national liberation movements and the socialist revolution as practically synonymous.

Precisely because they are nationalist these liberation

movements are so diverse in their practice and theory that no one of them can serve for the purposes of analysis as 'representative' of the rest (as the SPD could for the Second International). At the same time an account of all, or even a number of the ideological systems arising from these movements is ruled out on grounds of space. What is proposed, therefore, is to examine third world nationalist 'Marxism' in terms of what has been a central theme for almost all its incarnations — guerrilla war for national independence — and to do so with special reference to China and Cuba, the two 'purest' cases of this type of revolution. They have the added interest that Maoism began within Stalinism proper, developed its own independent strategy and then broke with Russia after it had achieved power, whereas Castroism began as non-Communist and non-Marxist, only moving into the Soviet camp and adopting a 'Marxist' ideology after it had achieved power. This procedure, inadequate as it is, should nonetheless be sufficient to reveal the essence of this kind of 'Marxism', its class basis.

Guerrilla warfare involves, in the first place, a relocation of the centre of the revolutionary struggle from the town to the countryside. The first 'Marxist' to take this step was Mao and he did it in response to the crushing of the Chinese working class by the Kuomintang in 1927. The motive was to save the remnants of the Chinese Communist Party from Chiang Kai-Shek's reign of terror in the cities[116] and this led Mao first to Kiangsi, and then, when this was attacked in force, on the incredible Long March to Yenan in the north west, one of the most backward and remote parts of China. This practical consideration, the greater difficulty experienced by the army and police in tracking down revolutionaries in the countryside, has remained of prime importance for advocates of guerrilla war. Thus Che Guevara, after commenting that 'illegal workers' movements face enormous dangers', writes: 'The situation in the open country is not so difficult. There, in places beyond the reach of the repressive forces, the inhabitants can be supported by armed guerrillas.'[117]

However, guerrilla warfare involves not only a shift in the location of the struggle but also a shift in its social content. The worker cannot become a guerrilla without ceasing to be a worker, and for the working class as a whole or even a substantial proportion of it rural guerrilla warfare is an evident impossibility. Which social class, then, is to replace the working class as the agent of revolution? The principal answer of the theorists of guerrilla war is: the peasantry.[118]

More than enough has already been said in the first part of this book to show that such a substitution of the peasantry for the proletariat is incompatible with Marxism, but it is worthwhile stressing that in no way is this just a matter of contradicting Marx's (and Lenin's) specific judgements on the revolutionary capacities of the peasants. For Marxism, as we have shown, the proletariat is fundamental. The working class is not the instrument of the revolution; on the contrary the revolution is the instrument of the working class, for the working class alone is linked to and embodies the forces and relations of production which can carry humanity forward to a higher, classless, stage of society.

Thus, just as it was impossible to insert socialism in one country into Marxism without necessitating a whole series of subsequent revisions, so the theory of peasant socialist revolution demolishes the entire structure of historical materialism. The peasant is the product not of capitalist but of pre-capitalist relations of production. If the peasantry is the socialist class then socialist revolution should have been possible at any time in the past thousand years. Capitalism and the industrial revolution would be unnecessary stages in human history and the determining role played by the development of the forces of production would be done away with completely. All that is needed is will power and correct ideas.

Precisely this notion manifests itself in the arguments of the Maoists, and their intellectual fellow travellers such as Charles Bettelheim, that socialism can be constructed in China or elsewhere however backward and impoverished the economic starting point, provided the political leadership is correct.[119] It appears also in the Castro-Guevara-Debray position that it is not necessary to wait for the objective conditions of revolution to mature, because the revolutionaries (guerrillas) can, themselves, create them.[120] The result is not Marxist materialism but rampant idealism.

One attempt to get round this problem, essayed by those such as Mao who felt some ideological loyalty to the Marxist tradition (refracted through Stalinism), was to speak always of 'proletarian leadership' of the peasantry.[121] But since the proletariat played no role at all in the Chinese Revolution ('it is hoped', wrote Mao in 1949, 'that workers and employees in all trades will continue to work and that business will operate as usual'[122]) this could only mean leadership by the 'proletarian' party. And since the Chinese Communist Party had practically no working class members,[123] this in turn could only mean leadership by 'proletarian' ideology. Once again we are back to idealism. Ideology, detached from its social base, is transferred onto another social class and supposedly remoulds it.

In fact extreme idealism and its vulgar version, the 'great man' theory, permeates Maoism. Examples range from the notion that the Soviet Union changed from the dictatorship of the proletariat to the dictatorship of the bourgeoisie with the change of leadership from Stalin to Krushchev, to the use of the terminology of class (bourgeois, landowner, and so on) as moral labels,[124] to the absurd cult of 'Mao Tse-tung thought' and the cult of Mao himself, 'the great helmsman', 'the sun that never sets'.[125]

It is important to note that whereas the cult of Stalin arose only after he was in power, the cult of Mao dates from before the conquest of power. This is because the revolutionary working class will tolerate no mystical leader cult and so Stalin had to smash the working class before he could impose his rule upon it, whereas peasant-based revolts typically view their leaders as semi-divine. Indeed one has only to think of the cults of Kim Il Sung, Ho Chi Minh, Fidel Castro, Che Guevara and others to see that this crude idealism is not only a common feature of national liberation 'Marxisms' but also a characteristic they share with openly non-Marxist nationalist movements (witness Gandhi, and the cult of Sun Yat-sen in the Kuomintang).

Marx is here stood on his head. It is not social being that determines social consciousness, but social consciousness (leadership) that determines social being. If the theorists of peasant guerrilla war were consistent, they would renounce Marxism altogether. Indeed if the central claims of these theorists — that guerrilla war is the road to socialism — are *true*, then Marxism is refuted in its most basic propositions. However, setting aside for the moment the idea that China, Cuba, Vietnam and so on are socialist, the idealist character of guerrilla-ist theories suggests immediately that the relationship between the guerrilla army and the peasantry is not at all what is claimed: for idealism itself has social roots — the existence of classes or strata who, living off the labour of others, come to believe it is their ideas that are the key to society.

To elucidate this problem it is necessary to return to Marx's analysis of the French peasantry in **The Eighteenth Brumaire of Louis Bonaparte**:

> The small-holding peasants form a vast mass, the members of which live in similar conditions but without entering into manifold relations with one another. Their mode of production isolates them from one another instead of bringing them into mutual intercourse . . . In so far as millions of families live under economic conditions of existence that separate their modes of life, their interests, and their culture from those of the other classes, and put them in hostile opposition to the latter, they form a class. In so far as there is merely a local interconnection among these small-holding peasants, and the identity of their interests begets no community, no national bond and no political organisation among them they do not form a class. They are consequently incapable of enforcing their class interests in their own name . . . They cannot represent themselves, they must be represented. Their representative must at the same time appear as their master, as an authority over them, as an unlimited governmental power that protects them against the other classes and sends them rain and sunshine from above.[126]

Marx has here put his finger on the fundamental characteristic of the peasantry, determined by the social conditions of its existence — its incapacity for self-emancipation. The peasantry can fight, and does so with extraordinary ferocity, but it cannot become the ruling class of society. The village can defeat the city in any number of battles, but it cannot win the war, for the village cannot run the city and that is where the productive forces are located. This was true of Wat Tyler in 1381, of Emiliano Zapata in Mexico, and of the countless peasant revolts that recur throughout Chinese history.[127] To cohere into a national political force the peasantry requires the leadership of an external urban-formed class, or section of a class. For Lenin, Marx and Trotsky this leadership was to be the working class, not by 'going to the countryside' but by fighting to overthrow the state in the cities. For Mao, Castro, Guevara and others, it was the cadres and command of the guerrilla army, who were drawn (and could only be drawn) almost exclusively from the urban intelligentsia.

What is the relationship between the leadership and the peasantry in the guerrilla war? First of all the rank and file of the guerrilla army will be overwhelmingly peasant in composition but only a tiny minority of the peasantry will participate in this way (in Cuba Castro's armed forces were a few thousand *at most*; in China the numbers were huge — 300,000 at the beginning of the Long March, 20,000 at its end, several million at the high point of the war — but still only a tiny fraction of China's 500 million peasants). The fact that the essence of guerrilla warfare is mobility and hit-and-run tactics makes this unavoidable.

And these same tactics ensure that the peasant guerrilla ceases to be a peasant and becomes a professional soldier, his actions and ideology detached from their class origin and re-moulded under military discipline by the middle class army command. The relationship is thus quite different from that between workers and intellectuals in a Leninist party, where the worker members remain workers and where the participation of intellectuals, necessary as it is, is conditional on their acceptance of the standpoint and discipline of the proletarian struggle.[128]

The relation of the guerrilla army to the peasantry as a whole is also quite different from the relationship between the Leninist party and the working class. The latter is concerned to lead the working class as a whole in a struggle to realise working class interests. The former is concerned to act *on behalf* of the mass of the peasantry. The guerrilla army needs the support of the peasantry certainly, and in return offers assistance, protection, and the bait of land reform. Guevara, unwittingly, gave a pure expression to the idealist elitism inherent in the strategy of guerrilla war:

> We have already described the guerrilla fighter as one who shares the longing of the people for liberation and who, once peaceful means are exhausted, initiates the fight and converts himself into an armed vanguard of the people. From the very beginning of the struggle he has the intention of destroying an unjust order and therefore an intention, more or less hidden, to replace the old with something new. We have also said already that in . . .

almost all countries with deficient economic development it is the countryside that offers ideal conditions for the fight. Therefore the foundation of the social structure that the guerrilla fighter will build begins with changes in the ownership of agrarian property.[129]

First comes the guerrilla fighter with his ideals of a just social order, 'a true priest of reform' as Guevara calls him; second the choice of terrain on military grounds; third the programme of agrarian reform. Guevara continues:

> The peasant must always be helped technically, economically, morally and culturally. The guerrilla fighter will be a sort of guiding angel who has fallen into the zone, helping the poor always and bothering the rich as little as possible in the first phases of the war.[130]

Similarly Mao's Red Army was under strict instructions in its dealing with the peasantry to: 'Be courteous and help out when you can. Return all borrowed articles. Replace all damaged articles . . . Pay for all articles purchased etc.'[131] What has to be grasped here is the power relationship between peasant and guerrilla that makes these moral injunctions necessary because in reality it is a continual temptation to behave otherwise. Imagine any workers' organisation, when sending its members to the factory gates, giving the orders: 'No mugging of the workers. No forcing them to buy our paper!'

The real basis of this elitism is not just the superior culture of the guerrilla command, nor even its possession of arms, but a divergence in class aims. The fundamental class aim of the peasantry is possession of the land. The fundamental aim of the revolutionary intelligentsia who form the guerrilla leadership is the capture of state power to achieve national liberation. The latter *uses* the former to propel *itself*, and not the peasantry, into power. That this applied to the army and party of Mao is shown by the way in which the Chinese Communist Party continually held back the spontaneous peasant struggle for land in order to maintain the national coalition in the war against Japan.[132]

The struggle of an oppressed nation for liberation, whether it is against formal colonial status as in Algeria or against a regime that is a client for imperialism as in Cuba, is progressive and must be supported, but it remains essentially a bourgeois democratic task. The nation state is the product of capitalism, and the mission of the proletariat is to overcome the division of the world into states. Consequently Marxist support for national liberation differs in motivation and method from bourgeois and petty bourgeois support. For the latter national liberation is a struggle to establish its territory, its own corner of the globe to rule, and is therefore regarded as an overriding end in itself, around which all 'national' classes should unite. For Marxists national liberation is only a *means*, a struggle to clear away national oppression since this constitutes an obstacle to the voluntary unification of the international working class in an eventual 'union of workers' republics'. It is therefore a struggle in which the proletariat must retain its class independence in order to carry the revolution beyond the social and national resting place with which the bourgeoisie and petty bourgeoisie will be content, in a process of permanent revolution.

From what we have seen it is clear that the strategy of guerrilla war (except as an ancillary to the workers' revolution) is incompatible with this proletarian internationalist perspective, and it is equally clear from their theory and their practice that none of the third world nationalist 'Marxists' have succeeded in transcending the nationalist position. This, apart from all other arguments, indicates that the class basis of their 'Marxism' is not the proletariat but the petty bourgeoisie.[133]

One further aspect of the problem remains to be considered. Once achieved, national liberation (if it is not transcended in international revolution) must be consolidated and maintained in the arena of fiercely competitive world capitalism. The petty bourgeois guerrilla elite propelled to power by peasant war thus finds itself in essentially the same position as the Bolshevik elite after the destruction of the working class in the Civil War, with the difference that it is not organically linked to the world working class through an international revolutionary party.[134] Therefore it has no choice but the Stalinist option, the struggle for economic growth through the accumulation of capital, based on the exploitation of the workers and peasants, which in turn means it must consolidate itself as a new ruling class.[135]

In this situation two things happen. Firstly the cult of the noble guerrilla sacrificing himself for his people becomes transformed into an ideology of working class (and peasant) self-sacrifice for the nation. Socialism becomes a doctrine of asceticism (dignified in the west by Bettelheim and others, as a critique of economism). Secondly, the seemingly radical, fluid structures of the nationalist revolution settle into the Stalinist mould of the bureaucratic one-party state. The parallelism of third world nationalism and Soviet Stalinism is thus more than a matter of shared ideological and organisational origins (present in China but not in Cuba), or necessary dependence on Russian aid (the case in Cuba but not in China since the early 1960s), it comes from a common class situation and common economic tasks.

To conclude. Third world nationalist 'Marxism', like Kautskyism and Stalinism, is in its origins an ideology not of proletarian revolution but of a section of the petty bourgeoisie which stands between labour and capital. In the case of Kautskyism and Stalinism it was the labour movement bureaucracy which had raised itself above its working-class base. In third world nationalism it is the middle class intelligentsia oppressed by imperialism. Unlike Kautskyism and Stalinism it has a certain 'revolutionary' content where the task of national liberation remains to be achieved. Like Stalinism in Russia and East Europe (but not Kautskyism or Stalinism in the west) it is able under certain conditions[136] to transform itself into the ruling class. As an ideology it is, in formal terms, much further from Marxism than either Kautskyism or Stalinism, and could only be accepted as a Marxism, or a version of Marxism because of the prior work of Stalinism in burying the genuine tradition under a mountain of distortion, and because of the extreme weakness of proletarian Marxism in the 1950s and 1960s.

Thus, for all their differences, Kautskyism, Stalinism and third world nationalism have much in common — above all a commitment to the national state (nationalism and state ownership) and rejection of the self-emancipation of the working class. These are features, arrived at by a different historical route, which Engels as far back as **Anti-Dühring** analysed as key characteristics of the ultimate stage of capitalist development:

> The modern state, no matter what its form, is essentially a capitalist machine, the state of the capitalists, the ideal personification of the total national capital. The more it proceeds to the taking over of the productive forces, the more does it actually become the national capitalist, the more citizens

does it exploit. The workers remain wage workers — proletarians. The capitalist relation is not done away with. It is rather brought to a head.[137]

What has happened, therefore, to these 'Marxisms' is that in abandoning the class positions of the proletariat they have ended up supporting the next stage of capitalism.

We have now completed our survey of the principal[138] transformations of Marxism since Marx's death, and can return to our starting point — the authentic Marxist tradition.

4
The authentic
Marxist tradition

The authentic Marxist tradition is not difficult to identify. It runs, from Marx and Engels, through the revolutionary left wing of the Second International (especially in Russia and Germany), reaches its height with the Russian Revolution and the early years of the Comintern, and is continued, in the most difficult circumstances possible, by the Left Opposition and the Trotskyist movement in the 1930s. The history and theory of this tradition has been so copiously analysed, defended and, where necessary, criticised by members of our own political tendency,[139] that only a few general observations are required here.

It is a tradition whose leading representatives, after its founders, are clearly Lenin, Luxemburg and Trotsky, but they are surrounded by many figures of only slightly lesser stature — Mehring, Zetkin, the early Bukharin, James Connolly, John McLean, Victor Serge, Alfred Rosmer, and so on, as well as hundreds of thousands of working class fighters.

It is a tradition which has sought always to unite theory and practice and therefore has never rested content with received wisdom or fixed dogma but has sought to apply Marxism to a changing world. Its most important contributions include theories of the party (Lenin), the mass strike (Luxemburg), permanent revolution (Trotsky), imperialism and the world economy (Luxemburg, Bukharin, Lenin and Trotsky), the counter-revolutionary role of Stalinism (Trotsky), fascism (Trotsky) and the restoration of the activist, dialectical element in Marxist philosophy (Lenin, Gramsci and Lukacs).

It has been for most of its existence, with the exception of the revolutionary years of 1917–23, the tradition of a tiny minority. This is unfortunate but unavoidable. The ruling ideas are the ideas of the ruling class and the mass of workers reach revolutionary consciousness only in revolutionary struggle. The permanent co-existence of a mass Marxist movement with capitalism is therefore impossible. Its very presence constitutes a threat to the capitalist order which, if it is not realised, will be removed. It is therefore a tradition whose advances and retreats reflect, in the last analysis, the advances and retreats of the working class.

It is not a monolithic tradition, but is characterised by vigorous debate (think of Luxemburg and Lenin on the party and the national question, or Lenin and Trotsky on the nature of the Russian Revolution, or the internal debates of the Bolshevik Party before and after 1917). Nor is it a tradition free from error (witness Trotsky's workers' state analysis of Russia). But it is united by the class basis on which it stands, the world working class,[140] and therefore has been in an important sense cumulative, with each Marxist generation building on the achievements of its forebears.

It is also *our* tradition. The traditions which the Socialist Workers Party in Britain and its international affiliates have sought to continue and develop over more than thirty years. Historical circumstances have not yet confronted us with the flames of war, revolution and counter-revolution. These are the conditions which put movements and theories to the test, revealing their inadequacies but also allowing them to achieve their full stature. Consequently, our achievements, theoretical and practical, appear small beer compared with those of our predecessors. Nonetheless, our major theoretical contributions and distinctive political positions — the state capitalist analysis of Stalinist states, the theory of deflected permanent revolution in the third world, the analysis of the arms economy boom and the new economic crisis, the critique of the trade union bureaucracy — have two things in common: they have been developed as responses to real problems faced by the workers' movement in the struggle to change the world, and they have taken as their starting point and emphasise as their conclusion the fundamental principle of Marxism — the self-emancipation of the working class. In **Left Wing Communism** Lenin wrote that 'correct revolutionary theory . . . assumes final shape only in close connection with the practical activity of a truly mass and truly revolutionary movement', and the achievement of that unity is, of course, the major task that faces us in the future.

Notes

1. Trotsky, **The Permanant Revolution and Results and Prospects** (New York, 1969) page 1.
2. Lukacs, **History and Class Consciousness** (London, 1971) page 1.
3. Ironically this reduction of Marxism to method has resurfaced recently in the speeches and writings of the Militant group in the British Labour Party (see for example Laurence Coates in **Socialist Worker**, 8 January 1983). For the Militant group, of course, it is not a question of a theoretical position but a political device to avoid embarrassing questions about revolution, the dictatorship of the proletariat and such like.
4. Lukacs, op. cit., page 1.
5. Trotsky, **In Defence of Marxism** (London, 1966) page 11.
6. Marx, **Preface to a Critique of Political Economy** in **Selected Works**, vol. 1 (Moscow 1969) page 503.
7. **Karl Marx: Selected Writings**, ed. D. McLellan (Oxford, 1978) page 63.
8. Ibid, page 63.
9. See the **Theses on Feuerbach**.
10. Engels, 'On the History of Early Christianity', in Marx and Engels, **Basic Writings on Politics and Philosophy** (New York, 1978) page 209.
11. Engels, **Anti-Dühring** (Peking, 1976) page 18.
12. **Karl Marx: Selected Writings**, op. cit., page 212.
13. Ibid., page 231.
14. Ibid., page 231.
15. **Towards a Critique of Hegel's Philosophy of Right: Introduction** (1844), ibid., page 73. We should also record the important role played by Engels at this time, on the basis of his experience of the English working class in Manchester.
16. Cited in Lenin, **What Is To Be Done?** (Moscow, 1969) page 40.
17. Ibid., page 32.
18. See J. Molyneux, **Marxism and the Party** (London, 1978) pages 46–50.
19. **Karl Marx: Selected Writings**, op. cit., page 229.
20. Marx to Weydemeyer, 5 March 1982, ibid., page 341.
21. Lenin, **Collected Works** (Moscow, 1962) vol. 25, page 412.
22. See K. Mannheim, **Ideology and Utopia** (London, 1976). Mannheim identified the independent intellectuals as the group most able to transcend their own social position and arrive at a synthesis of all differently socially-determined viewpoints.

Nigel Harris has noted the parallel between this notion and the 'explicit intellectual elitism of Kautsky (copied by the early Lenin)', **Beliefs in Society** (London, 1971) page 222.

23. See the second of Marx's Theses on Feuerbach. For an expanded version of this argument, with the necessary examples from the history of science, see Peter Binns, 'What are the tasks of Marxism in philosophy?' in **International Socialism** 2:17.

24. Provided that one understands 'objective' to mean, as Gramsci put it, 'humanly objective' and not 'an extra-historical and extra-human objectivity'. See Gramsci, **Selections from the Prison Notebooks** (London, 1971) pages 445–6.

25. Capitalist society, because it is based on alienated labour, takes on the appearance of an entity independent of men and women and beyond their control. The bourgeois sociologist Emile Durkheim, who regarded society as a moral reality external to the people who constituted it and advocated 'treating social facts as things', and the Stalinist philosopher Louis Althusser, who maintains that 'history is a process without subjects' both commit the same error of reification — an intellectual process which is merely the reflection of the material reality of alienation.

26. Though in the future it may be possible to broadly distinguish between the science of the bourgeois epoch and the science of the socialist epoch.

27. Lenin, **The Three Sources and Three Components of Marxism** (Moscow, 1981) page 7.

28. The bourgeoisie was not always in this position. In its early days, when it was struggling to establish itself as the ruling class, it did need to change society. Hence the great achievements of its theorists in philosophy (from Descartes to Hegel), politics (from Machiavelli to Rousseau) and economics (Smith and Ricardo). Hence Marx's famous distinction between the classical political economists, who made genuine scientific discoveries and the later 'hired prize-fighters' of the bourgeoisie.

29. Marx, **The German Ideology** (New York, 1947) page 40.

30. Lukacs, **Lenin** (London, 1970) page 9.

31. Ibid., page 90.

32. Marx and Engels, **Selected Works** (Moscow, 1962) vol. II, page 80.

33. Marx made the same methodological point when he wrote that 'Human anatomy contains the key to the anatomy of the ape.' Marx, **Grundrisse** (Harmondsworth, 1973) page 105.

34. For example: '(Men) begin to distinguish themselves from animals as soon as they begin to produce their means of subsistence.' **Karl Marx: Selected Writings**, op. cit., page 160.

35. Marx and Engels, **Selected Works**, op. cit., vol. II, page 91.

36. See Marx, **Critique of the Gotha Programme**, ibid., pages 27–28.

37. For the same reason support for national self-determination is not an automatic principle. There are instances where it runs counter to the overall interests of the working class and is therefore reactionary. Examples are: Slav nationalism in the nineteenth century, (in Marx's judgement) Serbian self-determination in World War I, Welsh and Scottish nationalism today.

38. Engels, 'Karl Marx', in Marx and Engels, **Selected Works**, op. cit., vol. II, page 164.

39. **Karl Marx: Selected Writings**, op. cit., pages 167–8.

40. 'There is no need of any great penetration to see from the teaching of materialism on the original goodness and equal intellectual endowment of men, the omnipotence of experience . . . the influence of environment on man . . . etc, how necessarily materialism is connected with communism and socialism.' **Karl Marx: Selected Writings**, op. cit., page 154.

41. Marx, 1st Thesis on Feuerbach.

42. Marx, 3rd Thesis on Feuerbach.

43. Ibid.

44. Karl Marx, **Early Writings**, ed. T. B. Bottomore (London, 1963) page 202.

45. Ibid., page 203.
46. Engels, 'Speech at the graveside of Karl Marx', Marx and Engels, **Selected Works**, op. cit., vol. II, page 167.
47. Marx, 'Preface to a Critique of Political Economy', **Karl Marx: Selected Writings**, op. cit., vol. II, page 167.
48. Ibid., page 214.
49. Marx, **Early Writings**, op. cit., page 69.
50. Ibid., page 120.
51. Ibid., page 59.
52. 'Break down' not in the sense of dissolving of its own accord, but in the sense of falling into profound crisis which creates the possibility of its overthrow.
53. It is not just a technical point, still less an accident, that **Capital** is built on the *labour* theory of value, or that the dual character of the commodity is derived from the dual character of labour (concrete and abstract labour).
54. Marx, **Early Writings**, op. cit., page 129.
55. Ibid., page 132.
56. Ibid., page 122.
57. Marx, **Capital** (London, 1974) page 582.
58. Marx, **Early Writings**, op. cit., page 604.
59. Marx, **Capital** vol. I, op. cit., page 604.
60. For many of these passages and a decisive refutation of the young Marx/old Marx thesis see Istvan Meszaros, **Marx's Theory of Alienation** (London, 1975) pages 217–53. For a flawed, but brilliant analysis of the centrality of alienated labour for the whole structure and logic of **Capital** see Raya Dunayevskaya, **Marxism and Freedom** (New York, 1964).
61. Marx, **Capital** vol. III (Moscow, 1966) page 250.
62. Lukacs, **History and Class Consciousness**, op. cit., pages 53–4 and pages 63–4 and Dunayevskaya, **Marxism and Freedom**, op. cit., page 143.
63. See Lucio Colleti, 'Marxism: Science or Revolution' in **From Rousseau to Lenin**.
64. Hilferding, Preface to **Finance Capital**, cited in P. Binns, op. cit. page 123.
65. Lenin, 'Our Programme', 1899.
66. Lenin, 'The Historical Destiny of the Teaching of Karl Marx', 1913.
67. This argument owes much to Nigel Harris' account of the transformations of Marxism in **Beliefs in Society**, op. cit., as do a number of arguments that follow.
68. That the seeds of reformism were present in the SPD from the beginning is evident from Marx's 'Critique of the Gotha Programme', and from Marx and Engels' 'Circular Letter', **Selected Correspondence** (Moscow, 1965) page 327.
69. Between 1900 and 1905 there was an average of only 1,171 strikes per year involving an average of 122,606 strikers per year. (Figures calculated from **Sozialgeschichtliches Arbeitsbuch, Materialien zur Statistik der Kaiserreichs 1870–1914** (Munich 1975) page 132.
70. Karl Kautsky, **The Class Struggle** (Erfurt Programme) (New York, 1971).
71. Ibid., page 7.
72. Ibid., page 8.
73. Ibid., page 88.
74. Ibid., page 7.
75. Ibid., page 159.
76. Marx, **The First International and After** (Harmondsworth, 1974) page 80.
77. Kautsky, **The Class Struggle**, op. cit.
78. Cited in M. Salvadori, **Karl Kautsky and the Socialist Revolution** (London, 1979) page 22.
79. Note the striking similarity between this and the strategy advocated by **Militant** inside the British Labour Party, with its notion of an 'enabling act' to permit the rapid nationalisation of the 'top 200 monopolies' — with the difference that Kautsky already had his mass party 'pledged to socialist policies', whereas **Militant** is still trying to get it.
80. Cited in M. Salvadori, op. cit., page 162.
81. Kautsky, **The Class Struggle**, op. cit., page 189.

82. Kautsky, cited in Lenin, **Marxism on the State** (Moscow, 1976) page 78.
83. See Rosa Luxemburg's brilliant analysis, **The Mass Strike, the Political Party and the Trade Unions**.
84. M. Salvadori, op. cit., page 108.
85. Ibid., page 111. Note the parallel with Kautsky's view that 'the problem of the dictatorship of the proletariat could be safely left to the future.'
86. Ibid., page 110.
87. For a further development of these themes, see John Molyneux, **Leon Trotsky's Theory of Revolution** (Brighton, 1981) Introduction.
88. If one is looking for a materialist explanation of why things turned out differently in Russia (not so much of Lenin's individual position but as to why that position had much more support than the stand taken by his fellow internationalists, Luxemburg and Liebknecht) then the absence of a developed labour bureaucracy in Russia is an important factor.
89. Cited in M. Salvadori, op. cit., page 324.
90. Lenin, **Collected Works** (Moscow, 1962) vol. 33, page 65.
91. I speak of choices because the Bolshevik cadre did have to choose between power and principles (those that vacillated lost both), but given the circumstances it was inevitable that the vast majority would choose power (provided that there was no revolution elsewhere to completely change the terms of the equation).
92. Cited in Isaac Deutscher, **Stalin** (Harmondsworth, 1976) page 272.
93. As an individual Stalin was remarkably fitted to fashioning this mask, as hypocrisy, lies and deception seem to have been, or become, an organic necessity for his personality.
94. See Marx's statement in **The German Ideology** that 'communism is only possible as the act of the dominant peoples "all at once" and simultaneously, which presupposes the universal development of productive forces and the world inter-course bound up with communism,' **Karl Marx: Selected Writings**, op. cit., page 171. See also Engels, **The Principles of Communism** (London. n.d.) page 15.
95. 'The final victory of socialism in a single country is of course impossible. Our contingent of workers and peasants which is upholding Soviet power is one of the contingents of a great world army.' Lenin, **Collected Works**, op. cit., vol. 26, pages 470–1. Most of Lenin's statements on socialism in one country are assembled by Trotsky in **The History of the Russian Revolution** (London 1977), Appendix II, pages 1219–57.
96. Cited in Trotsky, **The Third International After Lenin** (New York, 1970) page 36.
97. Stalin, **The Foundations of Leninism** (Peking, 1975) page 212.
98. See ibid., pages 28–9.
99. Trotsky, **The Revolution Betrayed** (London, 1967) page 212.
100. Engels' letter to Danielson, September 1892, cited in N. Harris, **Of Bread and Guns** (Harmondsworth, 1983) page 168.
101. Stalin, speech to business executives, 1931, cited in Isaac Deutscher, op. cit., page 328.
102. Lenin, **Collected Works**, op. cit., vol. 10, page 411.
103. See J. Stalin, **On the Opposition** (Peking, 1974) pages 595–619.
104. See J. Stalin, **Marxism and Problems of Linguistics** (Peking, 1976) page 48.
105. Engels, cited by Lenin in **The State and Revolution** (Peking, 1970) page 76.
106. See Isaac Deutscher, op. cit., pages 472–9.
107. Lenin, **The State and Revolution**, op. cit., page 6.
108. Trotsky, **The Third Internatonal After Lenin**, op. cit., page 72.
109. Other factors involved in this process were: Soviet Stalinism's declining need for western Stalinism once it had achieved nuclear parity; its loss of ideological authority after Kruschev's denunciation of Stalin in 1956, and the cumulative effects of the Yugoslav and Chinese schisms and the Hungarian and Czechoslovak revolts of 1956 and 1968.
110. There are even a few (though mostly these are left critics outside the Communist Parties) who revive the centrist notion of combining workers' councils and

parliament. This was the policy, under mass pressure, of the Mensheviks in 1917 and the USPD (left Social Democrats) in the German Revolution of 1919, and on both occasions was used to weaken the soviets and demobilise the working class.

111. Lenin, 'Theses on the National and Colonial Question', **Theses, Resolutions and Manifestos of the First Four Congresses of the Third International** (London, 1980) page 77.

112. Ibid., page 77.

113. Ibid., page 80.

114. Ibid., pages 80–81.

115. It should be noted that Stalinism adopted a completely different attitude to the oppressed nations in its own camp. Whether it was within the Soviet Union, or in Eastern Europe, or in its 'sphere of influence' (Afghanistan), *these* national movements were ruthlessly suppressed.

116. The difficulties of the Chinese Communist Party were compounded by the ultra-left 'third period' line of the Comintern at this time, which demanded the immediate preparation of armed uprisings. See N. Harris, **The Mandate of Heaven** (London, 1978) pages 16–18.

117. C. Guevara, **Guerrilla Warfare** (New York, 1967) page 16. Also 'the guerrilla fighter will carry out his action in wild places of small population.'

118. Though often this identification of the peasantry is disguised by the use of the term 'the people' in similar fashion to the Narodniks and Socialist Revolutionaries of Tsarist Russia.

119. 'What is happening in China proves that a low level of development of the productive forces is no obstacle to a socialist transformation of social relations.' C. Bettelheim, **Class Struggles in the USSR, 1917–1923** (Hassocks, 1976) page 42. For critiques of Bettelheim see N. Harris, 'Mao and Marx', **International Socialism** (first series) 89, and A. Callinicos, 'Maoism, Stalinism and the USSR', **International Socialism** (new series) 2:5.

120. 'It is not necessary to wait until all conditions for making revolution exist; the insurrection can create them.' C. Guevara, op. cit., page 15.

121. Unlike such advocates of peasant revolution as Frantz Fanon or Malcolm Caldwell who developed explicitly anti-proletarian theories. See F. Fanon, **The Wretched of the Earth** (Harmondsworth, 1970) especially page 86, and M. Caldwell, 'The Revolutionary Role of the Peasants', **International Socialism** (first series) 41.

122. Cited in T. Cliff, 'Permanent Revolution', **International Socialism** (first series) 61, page 21.

123. 'The Party admitted that workers comprised only 10 per cent of the membership in 1928, 3 per cent in 1929, 2.5 per cent in March 1930 . . . and virtually nothing at the end of it. From then until Mao's final victory the party had no industrial workers to speak of', ibid., page 20.

124. A good example of this is the denunciation of the Dung Xiao Ping faction in 1976 as 'leaders of the party linked to the bourgeoisie of our society, as well as landowners, rich peasants, counter-revolutionaries, bad elements, and badly re-educated bourgeois right wingers', to be followed in 1977 by the denunciation of the 'Gang of Four' as 'typical representatives in our party of landowners, rich peasants, counter-revolutionaries, bad elements, as well as other old and new bourgeois elements.' Cited in David Buxton, 'Another Goodbye to all that', **Radical Philosophy**, Summer 1979, page 32.

125. For evidence of this see Y. Gluckstein, **Mao's China** (London, 1957) page 378.

126. **Karl Marx: Selected Writings**, op. cit., pages 317–8.

127. For details see Y. Gluckstein, op. cit., pages 174–8.

128. This was one of the main points on which Lenin broke with the Mensheviks in 1903. See Lenin, **One Step Forward, Two Steps Back** (Moscow, 1969) page 66, and J. Molyneux, **Marxism and the Party**, op. cit., page 53.

129. C. Guevara, op. cit., page 43.

130. Ibid., page 43.

131. Some of the 'Eight Points' memorised and repeated daily by every Red Army soldier. The rest are all of a similar character.

132. For documentation of this see Y. Gluckstein, op. cit., pages 180–84, and N. Harris, **The Mandate of Heaven**, op. cit., pages 24–8.

133. How it came about that the petty bourgeoisie in some of the backward countries was able to play this role (contrary to the expectations of the theory of permanent revolution) is analysed in T. Cliff, 'Permanent Revolution', op. cit., and N. Harris, 'Perspectives for the Third World', **International Socialism** (first series) 42.

134. Another difference is that it is not encumbered by the legacy of institutionalised workers' power and therefore does not face the opposition that Stalinism faced, nor need it carry through the counter-revolution that Stalinism did. Hence its relatively benign appearance compared with the purges and camps of Russia in the 1930s.

135. See Lenin's comment on these two aspects of national liberation. 'Rousing the masses from feudal slumber, their struggle against all national oppression, for the sovereignty of nations, is progressive. Hence it is the bounden duty of a Marxist to uphold the most resolute and most consistent democratism in all parts of the national question. This task is mainly a negative one. But the proletariat cannot go beyond this in supporting nationalism, for beyond begins the "positive" activity of the bourgeoisie, which is striving to *fortify* nationalism.' Lenin, 'Critical remarks on the National Question', October–December 1913.

136. These being the extreme weakness and disintegration of the bourgeoisie proper and the passivity of the working class.

137. Marx and Engels, **Selected Works**, vol. II, op. cit., page 149.

138. It was originally intended to include an analysis of so-called 'Western Marxism' as identified by Perry Anderson, but, as so often, this essay has grown in the writing, and considerations of space now rule this out. Suffice it to say that with the exception of the early Lukacs and Gramsci (who arose in the Bolshevik tradition) all the leading figures of 'Western Marxism' (Marcuse and the Frankfurt school, Della Volpe and Colletti, Althusser, Poulantzas etc.), whatever their philosophical differences, are united by their rejection of international proletarian revolution, by their location within the upper ranks of the intelligentsia, and usually by their attachment to one or another form of Stalinism.

139. For example, T. Cliff, **Rosa Luxemburg** (London, 1959), T. Cliff, **Lenin** 4 vols (London, 1975–9), D. Hallas, **Trotsky's Marxism** (London, 1980), A. Callinicos, **The Revolutionary Ideas of Karl Marx** (London, 1983). These authors — and the present author — are all members of the British Socialist Workers Party.

140. It could be argued that where these errors were important, for example Luxemburg on the national question or Trotsky on Russia, they constituted a tendency to depart from the standpoint of the proletariat. However the point is that these errors constituted secondary rather than dominant features of these Marxists' total world outlook.

Appendix
Stalinism and Bolshevism
by Leon Trotsky

Reactionary epochs like ours not only disintegrate and weaken the working class and isolate its vanguard but also lower the general ideological level of the movement and throw political thinking back to stages long since passed through. In these conditions the task of the vanguard is, above all, not to let itself be carried along by the backward flow: it must swim against the current. If an unfavorable relation of forces prevents it from holding political positions it has won, it must at least retain its ideological positions, because in them is expressed the dearly paid experience of the past. Fools will consider this policy "sectarian." Actually it is the only means of preparing for a new tremendous surge forward with the coming historical tide.

The reaction against Marxism and Bolshevism

Great political defeats provoke a reconsideration of values, generally occurring in two directions. On the one hand the true vanguard, enriched by the experience of de-

Russian revolutionary Leon Trotsky wrote this article in 1936 to counter the arguments of his day—arguments that are still common on the left—that Stalinism was indistinguishable from Leninism. In reality, they were at opposite poles.

This version of "Stalinism and Bolshevism" comes from the Trotsky Internet Archive at www.marxists.org/archive/trotsky/index.htm.

feat, defends with tooth and nail the heritage of revolutionary thought and on this basis strives to educate new cadres for the mass struggle to come. On the other hand the routinists, centrists and dilettantes, frightened by defeat, do their best to destroy the authority of the revolutionary tradition and go backwards in their search for a "New World."

One could indicate a great many examples of ideological reaction, most often taking the form of prostration. All the literature if the Second and Third Internationals, as well as of their satellites of the London Bureau, consists essentially of such examples. Not a suggestion of Marxist analysis. Not a single serious attempt to explain the causes of defeat. About the future, not one fresh word. Nothing but clichés, conformity, lies and above all solicitude for their own bureaucratic self-preservation. It is enough to smell 10 words from some Hilferding or Otto Bauer to know this rottenness. The theoreticians of the Comintern are not even worth mentioning. The famous Dimitrov is as ignorant and commonplace as a shopkeeper over a mug of beer. The minds of these people are too lazy to renounce Marxism: they prostitute it. But it is not they that interest us now. Let us turn to the "innovators."

The former Austrian communist, Willi Schlamm, has devoted a small book to the Moscow trials, under the expressive title, The Dictatorship of the Lie. Schlamm is a gifted journalist, chiefly interested in current affairs. His criticism of the Moscow frame-up, and his exposure of the psychological mechanism of the "voluntary confessions," are excellent. However, he does not confine himself to this: he wants to create a new theory of socialism that would insure us against defeats and frame-ups in the future. But since Schlamm is by no means a theoretician and is apparently not well acquainted with the history of the development of socialism, he returns entirely to pre-Marxist socialism, and notably to its German, that is to its most backward, sentimental and mawkish variety. Schlamm denounces dialectics and the class struggle, not to mention the dictatorship of the proletariat. The problem of transforming society is reduced for him to the realization of certain "eternal" moral truths with which he would imbue mankind, even under capitalism. Willi Schlamm's attempts to save socialism by the insertion of the moral gland is greeted with joy and pride in Kerensky's review, Novaya Rossia (an old provincial Russian review now published in Paris); as the editors justifiably conclude, Schlamm has arrived at the principles of true Russian socialism, which a long time ago opposed the holy precepts of faith, hope and charity to the austerity and harshness of the class struggle. The "novel" doctrine of the Russian "Social Revolutionaries" represents, in its "theoretical" premises, only a return to the pre-March (1848!) Germany. However, it would be unfair to demand a more intimate knowledge of the history of ideas from Kerensky than from Schlamm. Far more important is the fact that Kerensky, who is in solidarity with Schlamm, was, while head of the government, the instigator of persecutions against the Bolsheviks as agents of the German general staff: organized, that is, the same frame-ups against which Schlamm now mobilizes his moth-eaten metaphysical absolutes.

The psychological mechanism of the ideological reaction of Schlamm and his like, is not at all complicated. For a while these people took part in a political movement that swore by the class struggle and appeared, in word if not in thought, to dialectical materialism. In both Austria and Germany the affair ended in a catastrophe. Schlamm draws the wholesale conclusion: this is the result of dialectics and the class struggle! And since the choice of revelations is limited by historical experience and…by personal knowledge, our reformer in his search for the word falls on a bundle of old rags which he valiantly opposes not only to Bolshevism but to Marxism as well.

At first glance Schlamm's brand of ideological reaction seems too primitive (from Marx…to Kerensky!) to pause over. But actually it is very instructive: precisely in its primitiveness it represents the common denominator of all other forms of reaction, particularly of those expressed by wholesale denunciation of Bolshevism.

"Back to Marxism"?

Marxism found its highest historical expression in Bolshevism. Under the banner of Bolshevism the first victory of the proletariat was achieved and the first workers' state established. No force can now erase these facts from history. But since the October Revolution has led to the present stage of the triumph of the bureaucracy, with its system of repression, plunder and falsification—the "dictatorship of the lie," to use Schlamm's happy expression—many formalistic and superficial minds jump to a summary conclusion: one cannot struggle against Stalinism without renouncing Bolshevism. Schlamm, as we already know, goes further: Bolshevism, which degenerated into Stalinism, itself grew out of Marxism; consequently one cannot fight Stalinism while remaining on the foundation of Marxism. There are others, less consistent but more numerous, who say on the contrary: "We must return Bolshevism to Marxism." How? To what Marxism? Before Marxism became "bankrupt" in the form of Bolshevism it has already broken down in the form of social democracy. Does the slogan "back to Marxism" then mean a leap over the periods of the Second and Third Internationals…to the First International? But it too broke down in its time. Thus in the last analysis it is a question of returning to the collected works of Marx and Engels. One can accomplish this historic leap without leaving one's study and even without taking off one's slippers. But how are we going to go from our classics (Marx died in 1883, Engels in 1895) to the tasks of a new epoch, omitting several decades of theoretical and political struggles, among them Bolshevism and the October Revolution? None of those who propose to renounce Bolshevism as an historically bankrupt tendency has indicated any other course. So the question is reduced to the simple advice to study *Capital*. We can hardly object. But the Bolsheviks, too, studied *Capital* and not badly either. This did not however prevent the degeneration of the Soviet state and the staging of the Moscow trials. So what is to be done?

Is Bolshevism responsible for Stalinism?

Is it true that Stalinism represents the legitimate product of Bolshevism, as all reactionaries maintain, as Stalin himself avows, as the Mensheviks, the anarchists, and certain left doctrinaires considering themselves Marxist believe? "We have always predicted this," they say. "Having started with the prohibition of other socialist parties, the repression of the anarchists, and the setting up of the Bolshevik dictatorship in the Soviets, the October Revolution could only end in the dictatorship of the bureaucracy. Stalin is the continuation and also the bankruptcy of Leninism."

The flaw in this reasoning begins in the tacit identification of Bolshevism, October Revolution, and Soviet Union. The historical process of the struggle of hostile forces is replaced by the evolution of Bolshevism in a vacuum. Bolshevism, however, is only a political tendency closely fused with the working class but not identical with it. And aside from the working class there exist in the Soviet Union a hundred million peasants, diverse nationalities, and a heritage of oppression, misery and ignorance. The state built up by the Bolsheviks reflects not only the thought and will of Bolshevism but also the cultural level of the country, the social composition of the population, the pressure of a barbaric past and no less barbaric world imperialism. To represent the process of degeneration of the Soviet state as the evolution of pure Bolshevism is to ignore social reality in the name of only one of its elements, isolated by pure logic. One has only to call this elementary mistake by its true name to do away with every trace of it.

Bolshevism, in any case, never identified itself either with the October Revolution or with the Soviet state that issued from it. Bolshevism considered itself as one of the factors of history, its "conscious" factor—a very important but not decisive one. We never sinned on historical subjectivism. We saw the decisive factor—on the existing basis of productive forces—in the class struggle, not only on a national scale but on an international scale.

When the Bolsheviks made concessions to the peasant tendency, to private ownership, set up strict rules for membership of the party, purged the party of alien elements, prohibited other parties, introduced the NEP [New Economic Policy—ed.], granted enterprises as concessions, or concluded diplomatic agreements with imperialist governments, they were drawing partial conclusions from the basic fact that had been theoretically clear to them from the beginning; that the conquest of power, however important it may be in itself, by no means transforms the party into a sovereign ruler of the historical process. Having taken over the state, the party is able, certainly, to influence the development of society with a power inaccessible to it before; but in return it submits itself to a 10 times greater influence from all other elements in society. It can, by the direct attack by hostile forces, be thrown out of power. Given a more drawn out tempo of development, it can degenerate internally while holding on to power. It is precisely this dialectic of the historical process that is not understood by those sectarian logicians who try to find in the decay of the Stalinist bureaucracy a crushing argument against Bolshevism.

In essence these gentlemen say: the revolutionary party that contains in itself no guarantee against its own degeneration is bad. By such a criterion Bolshevism is naturally condemned: it has no talisman. But the criterion itself is wrong. Scientific thinking demands a concrete analysis: how and why did the party degenerate? No one but the Bolsheviks themselves have, up to the present time, given such an analysis. To do this they had no need to break with Bolshevism. On the contrary, they found in its arsenal all they needed for the explanation of its fate. They drew this conclusion: certainly Stalinism "grew out" of Bolshevism, not logically, however, but dialectically; not as a revolutionary affirmation but as a Thermidorian negation. It is by no means the same.

Bolshevism's basic prognosis

The Bolsheviks, however, did not have to wait for the Moscow trials to explain the reasons for the disintegration of the governing party of the USSR. Long ago they foresaw and spoke of the theoretical possibility of this development. Let us remember the prognosis of the Bolsheviks, not only on the eve of the October Revolution but years before. The specific alignment of forces in the national and international field can enable the proletariat to seize power first in a backward country such as Russia. But the same alignment of forces proves beforehand that *without a more or less rapid victory of the proletariat in the advanced countries* the workers' government in Russia will not survive. Left to itself the Soviet regime must either fall or degenerate. More exactly; it will first degenerate and then fall. I myself have written about this more than once, beginning in 1905. In my *History of the Russian Revolution* (*cf*, "Appendix" to the last volume: "Socialism in one country") are collected all the statements on the question made by the Bolshevik leaders from 1917 until 1923. They all amount to the following: without a revolution in the West, Bolshevism will be liquidated either by internal counter-revolution or by external intervention, or by a combination of both. Lenin stressed again and again that the bureaucratization of the Soviet regime was not a technical question, but the potential beginning of the degeneration of the workers' state.

At the Eleventh Party Congress in March, 1922, Lenin spoke of the support offered to Soviet Russia at the time of the NEP by certain bourgeois politicians, particularly the liberal professor Ustrialov. "I am for the support of the Soviet power in Russia," said Ustrialov, although he was a Cadet, a bourgeois, a supporter of intervention—"because it has taken the road that will lead it back to an ordinary bourgeois state." Lenin prefers the cynical voice of the enemy to "sugary communistic nonsense." Soberly and harshly he warns the party of danger: "We must say frankly that the things Ustrialov speaks about are possible. History knows all sorts of metamorphoses. Relying on firmness of convictions, loyalty and other splendid moral qualities is anything but a serious attitude in politics. A few people may be endowed with splendid moral qualities, but historical issues are decided by vast masses, which, if the few don't suit them, may at times, treat them none too politely." In a word, the party is not the only factor of development and on a larger historical scale is not the decisive one.

"One nation conquers another," continued Lenin at the same congress, the last in which he participated…. "This is simple and intelligible to all. But what happens to the culture of these nations? Here things are not so simple. If the conquering nation is more cultured than the vanquished nation, the former imposes its culture on the latter, but if the opposite is the case, the vanquished nation imposes its culture on the conqueror. Has not something like this happened in the capital of the RSFSR [Russian Socialist Federation of Soviet Republics—ed.]? Have the 4,700 Communists (nearly a whole army division, and all of them the very best) come under the influence of an alien culture?" This was said in 1922, and not for the first time. History is not made by a few people, even "the best;" and not only that: these "best" can degenerate in the spirit of an alien, that is, a bourgeois culture. Not only can the Soviet state abandon the way of socialism, but the Bolshevik party can, under unfavorable historic conditions, lose its Bolshevism.

From the clear understanding of this danger issued the Left Opposition, definitely formed in 1923. Recording day by day the symptoms of degeneration, it tried to oppose to the growing Thermidor the conscious will of the proletarian vanguard. However, this subjective factor proved to be insufficient. The "gigantic masses" which, according to Lenin, decide the outcome of the struggle, become tired of internal privations and of waiting too long for the world revolution. The mood of the masses declined. The bureaucracy won the upper hand. It cowed the revolutionary vanguard, trampled upon Marxism, prostituted the Bolshevik party. Stalinism conquered. In the form of the Left Opposition, Bolshevism broke with the Soviet bureaucracy and its Comintern. This was the real course of development.

To be sure, in a formal sense Stalinism did issue from Bolshevism. Even today the Moscow bureaucracy continues to call itself the Bolshevik party. It is simply using the old label of Bolshevism the better to fool the masses. So much the more pitiful are those theoreticians who take the shell for the kernel and appearance for reality. In the identification of Bolshevism and Stalinism they render the best possible service to the Thermidorians and precisely thereby play a clearly reactionary role.

In view of the elimination of all other parties from the political field the antagonistic interests and tendencies of the various strata of the population, to a greater or less degree, had to find their expression in the governing party. To the extent that the political center of gravity has shifted from the proletarian vanguard to the bureaucracy, the party has changed its social structure as well as its ideology. Owing to the tempestuous course of development, it has suffered in the last 15 years a far more radical degeneration than did the social democracy in half a century. The present purge draws between Bolshevism and Stalinism not simply a bloody line but a whole river of blood. The annihilation of all the older generation of Bolsheviks, an important part of the middle generation which participated in the civil war, and that part of the youth that took up most seriously the Bolshevik traditions, shows not only a political but a thoroughly physical incompatibility between Bolshevism and Stalinism. How can this not be seen?

Stalinism and "state socialism"

The anarchists, for their part, try to see in Stalinism the organic product, not only of Bolshevism and Marxism, but of "state socialism" in general. They are willing to replace Bakunin's patriarchal "federation of free communes" by the modern federation of free Soviets. But, as formerly, they are against centralized state power. Indeed, one branch of "state" Marxism, social democracy, after coming to power became an open agent of capitalism. The other gave birth to a new privileged caste. It is obvious that the source of evil lies in the state. From a wide historical viewpoint, there is a grain of truth in this reasoning. The state as an apparatus of coercion is an undoubted source of political and moral infection. This also applies, as experience has shown, to the workers' state. Consequently it can be said that Stalinism is a product of a condition of society in which society was still unable to tear itself out of the straitjacket of the state. But this position, contributing nothing to the elevation of Bolshevism and Marxism, characterizes only the general level of mankind, and above all—the relation of forces between the proletariat and the bourgeoisie. Having agreed with the anarchists that the state, even the workers' state, is the offspring of class barbarism and that real human history will begin with the abolition of the state, we have still before us in full force the question: what ways and methods will lead, *ultimately*, to the abolition of the state? Recent experience bears witness that they are anyway not the methods of anarchism.

The leaders of the Spanish Federation of Labor (CNT), the only important anarchist organization in the world, became, in the critical hour, bourgeois ministers. They explained their open betrayal of the theory of anarchism by the pressure of "exceptional circumstances." But did not the leaders of German social democracy produce, in their time, the same excuse? Naturally, civil war is not peaceful and ordinary but an "exceptional circumstance." Every serious revolutionary organization, however, prepares precisely for "exceptional circumstances." The experience of Spain has shown once again that the state can be "denied" in booklets published in "normal circumstances" by permission of the bourgeois state, but the conditions of revolution leave no room for the denial of the state: they demand, on the contrary, the conquest of the state. We have not the slightest intention of blaming the anarchists for not having liquidated the state with the mere stroke of a pen. A revolutionary party, even having seized power (of which the anarchist leaders were incapable in spite of the heroism of the anarchist workers), is still by no means the sovereign ruler of society. But all the more severely do we blame the anarchist theory, which seemed to be wholly suitable for times of peace, but which had to be dropped rapidly as soon as the "exceptional circumstances" of the...revolution had begun. In the old days there were certain generals—and probably are now—who considered that the most harmful thing for an army was war. Little better are those revolutionaries who complain that revolution destroys their doctrine.

Marxists are wholly in agreement with the anarchists in regard to the final goal: the liquidation of the state. Marxists are "state-ist" only to the extent that one cannot achieve the liquidation of the state simply by ignoring it. The experience of Stalinism does not refute the teaching of Marxism but confirms it by inversion. The revolutionary doctrine which teaches the proletariat to orient itself correctly in situations and to profit actively by them, contains of course no automatic guarantee of victory. But victory is possible only through the application of this doctrine. Moreover, the victory must not be though of as a single event. It must be considered in the perspective of an historical epoch. The workers' state—on a lower economic basis and surrounded by imperialism—was transformed into the gendarmerie of Stalinism. But genuine Bolshevism launched a life and death struggle against the gendarmerie. To maintain itself Stalinism is now forced to conduct a direct *civil war* against Bolshevism under the name of "Trotskyism," not only in the USSR but also in Spain. The old Bolshevik party is dead but Bolshevism is raising its head everywhere.

To deduce Stalinism from Bolshevism or from Marxism is the same as to deduce, in a larger sense, counter-revolution from revolution. Liberal-conservative and later reformist thinking has always been characterized by this cliché. Due to the class structure of society, revolutions have always produced counter-revolutions. Does not this indicate, asks the logician, that there is some inner flaw in the revolutionary method? However, neither the liberals nor reformists have succeeded, as yet, in inventing a more "economical" method. But if it is not easy to rationalize the living historic process, it is not at all difficult to give a rational interpretation of the alternation of its waves, and thus by pure logic to deduce Stalinism from "state socialism," fascism from Marxism, reaction from revolution, in a word, the antithesis from the thesis. In this domain as in many others anarchist thought is the prisoner of liberal rationalism. Real revolutionary thinking is not possible without dialectics.

The political "sins" of Bolshevism as the source of Stalinism

The arguments of the rationalists assume at times, at least in their outer form, a more concrete character. They do not deduce Stalinism from Bolshevism as a whole but from its political sins. The Bolsheviks—according to Gorter, Pannekoek, certain German "Spartacists" and others—replaced the dictatorship of the proletariat with the dictatorship of the party; Stalin replaced the dictatorship of the party with the dictatorship of the bureaucracy, the Bolsheviks destroyed all parties except their own; Stalin strangled the Bolshevik party in the interests of a Bonapartist clique. The Bolsheviks compromised with the bourgeoisie; Stalin became its ally and support. The Bolsheviks recognized the necessity of participation in the old trade unions and in the bourgeois parliament; Stalin made friends with the trade union bureaucracy and bourgeois democracy. One can make such comparisons at will. For all their apparent effectiveness they are entirely empty.

The proletariat can take power only through its vanguard. In itself the necessity for state power arises from the insufficient cultural level of the masses and their heterogeneity. In the revolutionary vanguard, organized in a party, is crystallized the aspiration of the masses to obtain their freedom. Without the confidence of the class in the vanguard, without support of the vanguard by the class, there can be no talk of the conquest of power. In this sense the proletarian revolution and dictatorship are the work of the whole class, but only under the leadership of the vanguard. The Soviets are the only organized form of the tie between the vanguard and the class. A revolutionary content can be given this form only by the party. This is proved by the positive experience of the October Revolution and by the negative experience of other countries (Germany, Austria, finally, Spain). No one has either shown in practice or tried to explain articulately on paper how the proletariat can seize power without the political leadership of a party that knows what it wants. The fact that this party subordinates the Soviets politically to its leaders has, in itself, abolished the Soviet system no more than the domination of the conservative majority has abolished the British parliamentary system.

As far as the *prohibition* of other Soviet parties is concerned, it did not flow from any "theory" of Bolshevism but was a measure of defense of the dictatorship on a backward and devastated country, surrounded by enemies on all sides. For the Bolsheviks it was clear from the beginning that this measure, later completed by the prohibition of factions inside the governing party itself, signalized a tremendous danger. However, the root of the danger lay not in the doctrine or the tactics but in the material weakness of the dictatorship, in the difficulties of its internal and international situation. If the revolution had triumphed, even if only in Germany, the need of prohibiting the other Soviet parties would have immediately fallen away. It is absolutely indisputable that the domination of a single party served as the juridical point of departure for the Stalinist totalitarian regime. The reason for this development lies neither in Bolshevism nor in the prohibition of other parties as a temporary war measure, but in the number of defeats of the proletariat in Europe and Asia.

The same applies to the struggle with anarchism. In the heroic epoch of the revolution the Bolsheviks went hand in hand with genuinely revolutionary anarchists.

Many of them were drawn into the ranks of the party. The author of these lines discussed with Lenin more then once the possibility of allotting the anarchists certain territories where, with the consent of the local population, they would carry out their stateless experiment. But civil war, blockade and hunger left no room for such plans. The Kronstadt insurrection? But the revolutionary government could naturally not "present" to the insurrectionary sailors the fortress that protected the capital only because the re-actionary peasant-soldier rebellion was joined by a few doubtful anarchists. The concrete historical analysis of the events leaves not the slightest room for legends, built up on ignorance and sentimentality, concerning Kronstadt, Makhno and other episodes of the revolution.

There remains only the fact that the Bolsheviks from the beginning applied not only conviction but also com-pulsion, often to a most severe degree. It is also indis-putable that later the bureaucracy whom grew out of the revolution monopolized the system of compulsions in its own hands. Every stage of development, even such cata-strophic stages as revolution and counter-revolution, flows from the preceding stage, is rooted in it and carries over some of its features. Liberals, including the Webs, have al-ways maintained that the Bolshevik dictatorship repre-sented only a new edition of Tearooms. They close their eyes to such "details" as the abolition of the monarchy and the nobility, the handing over of the land to the peasants, the expropriation of capital, the introduction of the planned economy, atheist education, and so on. In exactly the same way liberal-anarchist thought closes its eyes to the fact that the Bolshevik revolution, with all its repres-sions, meant an upheaval of social relations in the interests of the masses, whereas Stalin's Thermidorian upheaval ac-companies the reconstruction of Soviet society in the inter-est of a privileged minority. It is clear that in the identification of Stalinism with Bolshevism there is not a trace of socialist criteria.

Questions of theory

One of the most outstanding features of Bolshevism has been its severe, exacting, even quarrelsome attitude towards the question of doctrine. The 26 volumes of Lenin's works will remain forever a model of the highest theoretical conscientiousness. Without this fundamental quality Bolshevism would never have fulfilled its historic role. In this regard Stalinism, coarse, ignorant and thoroughly empirical, is its complete opposite.

The Opposition declared more than 10 years ago in its program: "Since Lenin's death a whole set of new theories has been created, whose only purpose is to justify the Stalin group's sliding off the path of the international proletarian revolution." Only a few days ago an American writer, Liston M. Oak, who has participated in the Spanish revolution, wrote: "The Stalinists are in fact today the foremost revisionists of Marx and Lenin—Bernstein did not dare go half as far as Stalin in revising Marx." This is absolutely true. One must add only that Bernstein actually felt certain theoretical needs: he tried conscientiously to establish a correspondence between the reformist practices of social democracy and its program. The Stalinist bureaucracy, however, not only had nothing in common with Marxism but is in general foreign to any doctrine or system whatsoever. Its "ideology" is thoroughly permeated with police subjectivism; its practice is the empiricism of crude violence. In keeping with its essential interests the caste of usurpers is hostile to any theory: it can give an account of its social role neither to itself nor to anyone else. Stalin revises Marx and Lenin not with the theoretician's pen but with the heel of the GPU [Stalin's secret police—ed.].

Questions of morals

Complaints of the "immorality" of Bolshevism come particularly from those boastful nonentities whose cheap masks were torn away by Bolshevism. In petit-bourgeois, intellectual, democratic, "socialist," literary, parliamentary and other circles, conventional values prevail, or a conventional language to cover their lack of values. This large and motley society for mutual protection—"live and let live"—cannot bear the touch of the Marxist lancet on its sensitive skin. The theoreticians, writers and moralists, hesitating between different camps, thought and continue to think that the Bolsheviks maliciously exaggerate differences, are incapable of "loyal" collaboration and by their "intrigues" disrupt the unity of the workers' movement. Moreover, the sensitive and touchy centrist has always thought that the Bolsheviks were "calumniating" him—simply because they carried through to the end for him his half-developed thoughts: he himself was never able to. But the fact remains that only that precious quality, an uncompromising attitude towards all quibbling and evasion, can educate a revolutionary party which will not be taken unawares by "exceptional circumstances."

The moral qualities of every party flow, in the last analysis, from the historical interests that it represents. The moral qualities of Bolshevism—self-renunciation, disinterestedness, audacity and contempt for every kind of tinsel and falsehood (the highest qualities of human nature!)—flow from revolutionary intransigence in the service of the oppressed. The Stalinist bureaucracy imitates also in this domain the words and gestures of Bolshevism. But when "intransigence" and "flexibility" are applied by a police apparatus in the service of a privileged minority they become a force of demoralization and gangsterism. One can feel only contempt for these gentlemen who identify the revolutionary heroism of the Bolsheviks with the bureaucratic cynicism of the Thermidorians.

Even now, in spite of the dramatic events in the recent period, the average philistine prefers to believe that the struggle between Bolshevism ("Trotskyism") and Stalinism concerns a clash of personal ambitions, or, at best, a conflict between two "shades" of Bolshevism. The crudest expression of this opinion is given by Norman Thomas, leader of the American Socialist Party: "There is little reason to believe," he writes (*Socialist Review*, September 1937, p. 6), "that if Trotsky had won (!) instead of Stalin, there would be an end of intrigue, plots, and a reign of fear in Russia." And this man considers himself... a Marxist. One would have the same right to say: "There is little reason to believe that if instead of Pius XI, the Holy See were occupied by Norman I, the Catholic Church would have been transformed into a bulwark of socialism." Thomas fails to understand that it is not a question of antagonism between Stalin and Trotsky, but of an antagonism between the bureaucracy and the proletariat. To be sure, the governing stratum of the USSR is forced even now to adapt itself to the still not wholly liquidated heritage of revolution, while preparing at the same time through direct civil war (bloody "purge"— mass annihilation of the discontented) a change of the social regime. But in Spain the Stalinist clique is already acting openly as a bulwark of the bourgeois order against socialism. The struggle against the Bonapartist bureaucracy is turning before our eyes into class struggle: two worlds, two programs, two moralities. If Thomas thinks that the victory of the socialist proletariat over the infamous caste of oppressors would not politically and morally regenerate the Soviet regime, he proves only that for all his reservations, shufflings and pious sighs he is far nearer to the Stalinist bureaucracy than to the workers. Like other exposers of Bolshevik "immorality," Thomas has simply not grown to the level of revolutionary morality.

The traditions of Bolshevism and the Fourth International

The "lefts" who tried to skip Bolshevism in their return to Marxism generally confined themselves to isolated panaceas: boycott of parliament, creation of "genuine" Soviets. All this could still seem extremely profound in the heat of the first days after the war. But now, in the light of most recent experience, such "infantile diseases" have no longer even the interest of a curiosity. The Dutchmen Gorter and Pannekoek, the German "Spartacists," the Italian Bordigists, showed their independence from Bolshevism only by artificially inflating one of its features and opposing it to the rest. But nothing has remained either in practice or in theory of these "left" tendencies: an indirect but important proof that Bolshevism is the *only* possible form of Marxism for this epoch.

The Bolshevik party has shown in action a combination of the highest revolutionary audacity and political realism. It established for the first time the correspondence between the vanguard and the class which alone is capable of securing victory. It has proved by experience that the alliance between the proletariat and the oppressed masses of the rural and urban petit bourgeoisie is possible only through the political overthrow of the traditional petit-bourgeois parties. The Bolshevik party has shown the entire world how to carry out armed insurrection and the seizure of power. Those who propose the abstraction of the Soviets from the party dictatorship should understand that only thanks to the party dictatorship were the Soviets able to lift themselves out of the mud of reformism and attain the state form of the proletariat. The Bolshevik party achieved in the civil war the correct combination of military art and Marxist politics. Even if the Stalinist bureaucracy should succeed in destroying the economic foundations of the new society, the experience of planned economy under the leadership of the Bolshevik party will have entered history for all time as one of the greatest teachings of mankind. This can be ignored only by sectarians who, offended by the bruises they have received, turn their backs on the process of history.

But this is not all. The Bolshevik party was able to carry on its magnificent "practical" work only because it illuminated all its steps with theory. Bolshevism did not create this theory: it was furnished by Marxism. But Marxism is a theory of movement, not of stagnation. Only events on such a tremendous historical scale could enrich the theory itself. Bolshevism brought an invaluable contribution to Marxism in its analysis of the imperialist epoch as an epoch of wars and revolutions; of bourgeois democracy in the era of decaying capitalism; of the correlation between the general strike and the insurrection; of the role of the party, Soviets and trade unions in the period of proletarian revolution; in its theory of the Soviet state, of the economy of transition, of fascism and Bonapartism in the epoch of capitalist decline; finally in its analysis of the degeneration of the Bolshevik party itself and of the Soviet state. Let any other tendency be named that has added anything essential to the conclusions and generalizations of Bolshevism. Theoretically and politically Vandervilde, De Brouckere, Hilferding, Otto Bauer, Leon Blum, Zyromski, not to mention Major Attlee and Norman Thomas, live on the tattered leftovers of the past. The degeneration of the Comintern is most crudely expressed by the fact that it has dropped to the theoretical level of the Second International. All the varieties of intermediary groups (Independent Labour Party of Great Britain, POUM and their like) adapt every week new haphazard fragments of Marx and Lenin to their current needs. Workers can learn nothing from these people.

Only the founders of the Fourth International, who have made their own the whole tradition of Marx and Lenin, take a serious attitude towards theory. Philistines may jeer that 20 years after the October victory the revolutionaries are again thrown back to modest propagandist preparation. The big capitalists are, in this question as in many others, far more penetrating than the petit bourgeois who imagine themselves "socialists" or "communists." It is no accident that the subject of the Fourth International does not leave the columns of the world press. The burning historical need for revolutionary leadership promises to the Fourth International an exceptionally rapid tempo of growth. The greatest guarantee of its further success lies in the fact that it has not arisen away from the great historical road, but has organically grown out of Bolshevism.

About Haymarket Books

We believe that activists need to take ideas, history and politics into the many struggles for social justice today. Learning the lessons of past victories as well as defeats can arm a new generation of fighters for a better world.

As Karl Marx said, "The philosophers have merely interpreted the world; the point however is to change it."

We take inspiration and courage from our namesakes, the Haymarket Martyrs, who gave their lives fighting for a better world. Their struggle for the eight-hour day in 1886, which gave us May Day, the international workers' holiday, reminds workers around the world that ordinary people can organize and struggle for their own liberation. These struggles continue today across the globe—struggles against oppression, exploitation, hunger and poverty.

It was August Spies, one of the Martyrs who was targeted for being an immigrant and an anarchist, who predicted the battles being fought to this day. "If you think that by hanging us you can stamp out the labor movement," Spies told the judge, "then hang us. Here you will tread upon a spark, but here, and there, and behind you, and in front of you, and everywhere, the flames will blaze up. It is a subterranean fire. You cannot put it out. The ground is on fire upon which you stand.

Haymarket Books
PO Box 180165
Chicago, IL 60618

773.583.7884

www.haymarketbooks.org

Other titles from
Haymarket Books

The Struggle for Palestine
Edited by Lance Selfa
ISBN 1931859000 2002 256 pages

With U.S. approval, Israel has unleashed a savage war against the Palestinians. Israel aims for nothing less than to force the Palestinian people to surrender their just demands for self-determination.

At the same time, the Palestinian movement faces its own crossroads. With the Oslo "peace process" exposed as a sham, increasing numbers of Palestinians and their supporters are asking how we can win the liberation of Palestine.

Contributors to *The Struggle for Palestine* offer a fresh analysis of the fight against Zionism—and make the case for a secular, democratic state in all of Palestine.

The Forging of the American Empire
By Sindney Lens
ISBN 0745321003 2003 465 pages

This is the story of a nation—the United States—that has conducted more than 160 wars and other military ventures while insisting that it loves peace.

In the process, the U.S. has forged a world empire while maintaining its innocence of imperialistic designs.

From Mexico to Lebanon, from China to the Dominican Republic, from Nicaragua to Vietnam, the U.S. has intervened regularly in the affairs of other nations.

Yet the myth that Americans are benevolent, peace-loving people who will fight only to defend the rights of others lingers on.

Excesses and cruelties, though sometimes admitted, usually are regarded as momentary aberrations.

In this comprehensive history of American imperialism, Sidney Lens punctures the myth once and for all by showing how the U.S., from the time it gained its own independence, has used every available means—political, economic, and military—to dominate other peoples.

Trotsky's Marxism and Other Essays

By Duncan Hallas

ISBN 1931859035   2003   206 pages

No serious attempt to understand the tragedy of the Russian Revolution—and its relevance to the building of socialism today—can ignore the unique contribution made by Leon Trotsky.

Leon Trotsky was one of the major architects of the October Revolution of 1917 and an organizer of the Red Army. Ironically, it also fell to him to chronicle and analyze the degeneration and destruction of socialism in Russia under Stalin's regime.

In this introduction to the politics of Leon Trotsky, Duncan Hallas analyzes four major strands in Trotsky's writings.

First, the theory of "permanent revolution," in which Trotsky elaborated a scenario for the revolution of 1917 and for understanding subsequent political developments in the underdeveloped world.

Second, the first sustained attempt at a materialist analysis of the rise of Stalinism, which Trotsky spent years seeking to understand—and against which he courageously organized international opposition.

Third, Trotsky's analysis of the strategy and tactics of mass revolutionary parties in a wide variety of situations, particularly his theory of the "united front."

Fourth, his views on the relationship between the revolutionary socialist party and the working class in periods of mass upheaval as well as in periods of decline.

In addition, *Trotsky's Marxism and Other Essays* includes essential writings by Duncan Hallas about the development of Trotskyism after Trotsky's assassination by Stalin's agents in 1940 and the need for an assessment of that tradition in building today's struggles.

The Lost Revolution

By Chris Harman

ISBN 1931859066   2003   331 pages

Revolutions that are defeated are soon forgotten.

Yet of all the upheavals after the First World War, it was the events in Germany that prompted British Prime Minister Lloyd George to write:

"The whole existing order, in its political, social and economic aspects, is questioned by the masses from one end of Europe to another."

Here was a great revolutionary upheaval in an advanced industrial country—in the heart of Europe.

Without an understanding of the defeat, the great barbarisms that swept Europe in the 1930s cannot be understood—for the swastika first entered modern history on the uniforms of the German counter-revolutionary troops of 1918-23, and because of the defeat in Germany, Russia fell into the isolation that gave Stalin his road to power.